TIMEX/SINCLAIR®
INTERFACING

James M. Downey is a professor in the Department of Physiology, College of Medicine, at the University of South Alabama.

Don Rindsberg is president of The Bit Stop, a computer consulting firm located in Mobile, Alabama.

TIMEX/SINCLAIR™ INTERFACING

James M. Downey
Don Rindsberg

A SPECTRUM BOOK

PRENTICE-HALL, INC. Englewood Cliffs, NJ 07632

Library of Congress Cataloging in Publication Data

Downey, James M.
    Timex/Sinclair interfacing.

    ''A Spectrum Book.''
    Includes index.
    1. Sinclair ZX80 (Computer) 2. Sinclair ZX81
(Computer) 3. Timex 1000 (Computer) 4. Computer
interfaces. I. Rindsberg, Don. II. Title.
QA76.8.S624D68. 1983   001.64   83-4602
ISBN 0-13-921759-2
ISBN 0-13-921742-8 (pbk.)

A SPECTRUM BOOK

10 9 8 7 6 5 4 3 2 1

Printed in the United States of America

Editorial/production supervision by Cyndy Lyle Rymer
Manufacturing buyer Christine Johnston
Cover design by Hal Siegel

ISBN 0-13-921759-2

ISBN 0-13-921742-8 {PBK.}

Prentice-Hall International, Inc., *London*
Prentice-Hall of Australia Pty. Limited, *Sydney*
Prentice-Hall of Canada Inc., *Toronto*
Prentice-Hall of India Private Limited, *New Delhi*
Prentice-Hall of Japan, Inc., *Tokyo*
Prentice-Hall of Southeast Asia Pte. Ltd., *Singapore*
Whitehall Books Limited, *Wellington, New Zealand*
Editora Prentice-Hall do Brasil Ltda., *Rio de Janeiro*

CONTENTS

3

CREATING SPACE FOR EXPANSION IN THE SINCLAIR   23

4

PARALLEL OUTPUT PORTS   37

5

PARALLEL INPUT PORTS   53

6

HANDLING ANALOG SIGNALS   65

7

JOYSTICKS   83

8

MEMORY EXPANSION   97

9

INTERFACING PRINTERS   105

10

THE SINCLAIR AS A DUMB TERMINAL   123

11

LEVEL-SHIFTING FOR THE PRINTER AND THE DUMB TERMINAL 135

PREFACE

With the advent of the Sinclair computer, many would-be computer fans have finally taken the plunge into what has to be America's newest and most unusual avocation: personal computing. The interest in computing cuts across traditional class and even sex lines and has attracted people from all walks of life. In their quest to explore the capabilities of the Sinclair, the aficionados have diverged into software projects (either in BASIC or machine language), games, and hardware development. It is for those who have an interest in hardware that this book was written. We have attempted to compile the very basics of microprocessor interfacing in this volume so that even the greenest of beginners can understand, build, and, it is hoped, go on to actually design useful peripherals for Sinclair computers. In effort to make this volume self-contained, we have included chip data for all the integrated circuits (ICs) that are mentioned, construction techniques for digital circuits, and even plans for a logic probe with which you can troubleshoot the projects. In addition, we have attempted to employ only parts that are inexpensive and readily available. When hard-to-find items are described, the text includes ordering information.

A particular feature of this presentation is that the material actually transcends the Sinclair computer. The principles of interfacing described here apply to virtually all microprocessors; as a result, the design skills garnered in the simple environment of your Sinclair can be applied with only minor modifications to the much more complex microcomputers or even minicomputers. For this reason we have tried to explain in detail the theoretical workings of these projects and have included some simple teaching experiments that illustrate these principles.

The reader should be aware that all the projects described in this book have been tested by the authors and do work. It is possible, however, that you might inadvertently miswire one of these projects in such a way that damage might result to your Sinclair computer. Since we cannot prevent that possibility, you must be advised that the potential always exists with any hardware modification or addition to your computer and that the authors or the publisher cannot be held liable for such damage.

A few of the projects involve 110-volt house current for their operation. In constructing these projects, you should be sure that the 110-volt wires are thoroughly insulated against accidental contact with people or the computer-associated wiring. Remember that 110 volts can be lethal! The publisher and authors cannot be responsible for the misapplication of these projects.

Although this book contains projects for the Timex 1000 and the ZX81, we have made every effort to make the projects compatible with the 4K XZ80 and its upgraded version with the 8K ROM. We have not tested these projects on the Micro Ace version of the Sinclair, but most of them should work on it with little or no modification. At the time of this writing (October 1982) Sinclair has really had only one version of its 8K ROM in production. We, of course, cannot anticipate future software changes or, for that matter, even changes in the hardware design. Therefore we must advise the reader to be aware of the possibility of change, especially on machines built much later than the present publication date. We hope that you have as much fun building and using the projects in this book as we did designing and describing them.

Acknowledgments

We wish to convey our gratitude to all those who helped us in our preparation of this book. We especially wish to thank Ron Phillips for his disassembly of the Sinclair ROM and for assembling the machine programs presented here. The fine artwork in these pages is the handwork of Bill Isherwood. Finally, we offer our thanks to Leigh Cosper and Sandy Worley for their efforts in preparing this manuscript. Their infinite patience with our struggle with the English language has been remarkable.

1

FUNDAMENTALS OF MICROCOMPUTERS

Your Sinclair machine is a true digital computer; despite its bargain-basement price tag, it uses one of the most powerful 8-bit microprocessor chips available today: Zilog's Z80. This microprocessor can execute over 400 separate instructions and will execute most of them in less than 4 microseconds each. What is innovative about Sinclair computers is that they have been carefully designed to reduce the number of components to an absolute minimum. This reduction was achieved through very efficient hardware design and innovative software in the Sinclair Read-Only Memories (ROMs), which fully utilize the Z80's capabilities.* Although these computers cannot compare in power with the more expensive personal computers on the market that support disk drives for mass storage, Sinclair's interpreted BASIC is powerful and there are many tasks for which the Sinclair is ideally suited. Before we proceed with specific interfacing projects, we feel that it will be of immense help for the reader to understand what the Z80 is and how it is implemented in Sinclair computers.

*Hardware refers to the actual circuitry in the computer, whereas software refers to the program that the computer executes. Often the same function can be achieved by simpler hardware and more complex software. Although this "trade-off" increases development costs, it greatly decreases the production cost and is, therefore, a desirable design goal.

FIGURE 1-1
Z80 pinouts

Package Configuration

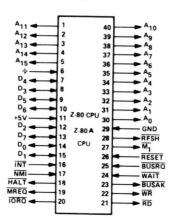

Package Outline

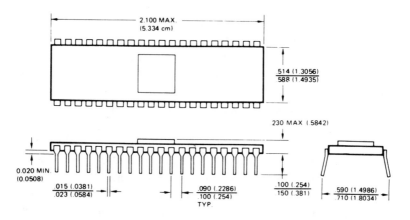

*Dimensions for metric system are in parentheses

What is a microcomputer?

The Z80 microprocessor serves several functions. It can perform arithmetic and logical operations internally. It can also direct data to and from memory external to the Z80. Finally, and perhaps most importantly, it can also fetch and execute a sequence of commands stored in memory, which we refer to as the *program*.

Binary bits and bytes

The Z80 microprocessor does all its arithmetic in a binary- (or base-2) number system. Because binary systems use only 2 digits—1 and 0—it is easy to implement them in digital electronics. The 1 represents the high state, +5 volts in the Z80, and the 0 represents the low state, 0 volts. In order to express numbers greater than 0 or 1, the computer carries the data as a multiple-digit binary number that we refer to as a *word*. Obviously each digit in the computer must be represented by a discrete electrical circuit. The Z80 has 8 such circuits for data manipulation and therefore is said to have an 8-bit word length, with each bit standing for a binary digit. If you will recall, your high-school mathematics course taught that each successive digit in any number system represented the base raised to a higher power. The following table shows how bit 0 represents 2 to the 0 power, or 1, and is thus the 1's digit. Bit 1 is 2 to the first power, or 2. Bit 1 thus becomes the 2's digit. Bit 2 becomes 2 to the second power or the 4's digit and so on to bit 7. Bit 7 is 2 to the seventh power or the 128's digit.

Power of 2	7	6	5	4	3	2	1	0
Result	128	64	32	16	8	4	2	1
Bit # in the Z80	7	6	5	4	3	2	1	0

Thus the 8-bit number 10010110 represents one 128, no 64s, no 32s, one 16, no 8s, one 4, one 2, and no 1s. The sum of these numbers is 150. Thus 10010110 in binary is equivalent to 150 in decimal notation. One obvious problem with an 8-bit data word is that 255 in decimal notation is the largest number that can be represented. Larger numbers require more binary bits. Clearly your Sinclair computer can work with numbers larger than 255. It simply does it internally by representing the data with several 8-bit words. When several words are used, however, great care must be taken to keep track of which word represents which part of the number. Most large computers use a 16-bit rather than an 8-bit word length, which makes programming much easier. Since these computers sell for thousands of dollars and often fill the better part of a room, 16 sets of logic circuits do not present much of a problem in the big machines. Microprocessors, however, must sell for under $20 and be small enough to fit in your pocket. Thus the compromise was made to limit the number of bits to only 8.

The 8-bit word length is often referred to as a *byte*. IBM introduced the term byte to refer to one-half of their 16-bit word since they had several instructions that would manipulate just 8 bits at a time. Because many of the early micro users had trained on the big 16-bit machines, they referred to the 8-bit word as a byte. The name has stuck, so even though 8 bits represent a full word in the Z80, those 8 bits are usually called a byte rather than a word in microprocessor jargon.

Computer anatomy

The Sinclair computer, like any computer, consists of 3 basic parts—the central processor unit, the memory, and the input/output (often abbreviated to I/O) devices. The central processor unit is, of course, the Z80 chip, which we have already discussed. Now let's examine the other two components.

Memory

Memory in your Sinclair computer is important for two reasons—it is the place where the program is stored, and it provides locations for information to be temporarily stored until the computer can process it. Memory in the Z80 is organized into a series of 8-bit bytes to or from which the computer can either deposit or retrieve 8 bits of information at a time. The Z80 selects a specific memory location by placing its binary code on the 16 address lines that emanate from the Z80 chip. Since there are 16 such lines, 2^{16} or 65,536 individual locations can be uniquely addressed. Although the Z80 can address 65,536 words of memory, only a small fraction of this space is filled in Sinclair computers. This space ranges from 5,020 bytes in the ZX80 to 10,250 bytes in the Timex 1000. The remaining space can, happily, be used for expansion.

Memory is divided into two types—read-write (often called RAM, which stands for *random-access memory*) and *read-only memory*, or ROM. The former, as its name implies, can either be written to or read from. RAM is necessary in your computer because it is needed to store temporary data. When you enter a BASIC program, it is held in RAM, and as long as you do not unplug the power, the computer will be able to remember your program. This quality brings up an important point about RAM. One of the technological developments that made personal micro-computers, if not possible, at least affordable, was the introduction of semiconductor memory. Originally computers used expensive core-type memory. Core type of memory operated on a principle of magnetizing small rings called cores. Once magnetized, a core would stay magnetized even if the power was turned off. That, however, is not true of cheap semiconductor memory. All data is lost when the power is interrupted, even if only briefly. A computer can only operate if a program is resident in memory. In the core-based computers, a start-up program called a *bootstrap* was entered through switches on a control panel. Once entered, the bootstrap would then be there every time the computer was turned on. When the first microcomputers, such as the Altair, appeared on the market, they had front panels as well, and it was necessary to key in the bootstrap every time the system was fired up. This inconvenience was overcome by the rapid development of *read-only memory*, or ROM as it is better known.

ROMs are programmed once and retain their data thereafter. Although the computer cannot deposit data in a ROM, it can execute programs that are stored in a ROM. By placing the bootstrap program in an inexpensive ROM, it no longer was necessary to key it in through the control panel. Not only was this change a time saver, but it proved to be economical as well because the expensive control panel became unnecessary. Today the control panel for most microcomputer systems consists of a single off-on switch. Your Sinclair computer comes with either 4,000 or 8,000 words of read-only memory, depending on which model you have. When the Z80 is first started, it automatically starts executing the program beginning at location 0, the first word of memory. That is where the ROM is located. The ROM program first does a memory test to find out how much RAM is present in that particular model; then it starts the BASIC interpreter.

Finally it should be mentioned that memory size is usually expressed in Ks. One K (short for the Greek word for a thousand, *Kilo*) in computer jargon refers to 1024. This is 2^{10} and a convenient unit of memory size. Thus when someone refers to the ZX80's 4K ROM, they mean that it has 1024×4 or 4096 words of read-only memory.

I/O Devices

The third part of the computer that you should be aware of is the *I/O* (input/output) section. Regardless of how powerful a computer might be, it is only useful if it has some means of communicating with the external world. The Sinclair computer can communicate with us via the TV screen and the keyboard. The TV screen is an output device. Similarly the keyboard is an input device. Your Sinclair is not limited, however, to only these forms of communication. For example, it can also communicate with a tape recorder to save programs. Many other forms of communication are possible with your Sinclair computer. It can turn lights off and on in your house, receive and send Morse code over a ham-radio set, measure the temperature in your garden, and perform a variety of other tasks, if the proper I/O devices are incorporated into the computer. The way such devices are incorporated is called *interfacing*. The principles of interfacing are actually quite simple and easily grasped, as you will find out in the succeeding chapters.

There are two ways in which I/O devices can be interfaced to the Z80. The first is as a true I/O device using the $\overline{\text{IOREQ}}$* signal from the Z80 to control the data transfer. The other is to interface the device as if it were memory. In the latter mode the $\overline{\text{MREQ}}$ signal must be used rather than the IOREQ. Although the former method is preferable in most systems since the I/O devices do not use valuable memory space, it is not preferable in the Sinclair. In Sinclair computers, there is no command available to BASIC to access I/O devices. BASIC does, however, have two commands (PEEK and POKE) that can access memory. Thus if an I/O device is interfaced to the Sinclair as if it were a memory location, you will be able to send data to it with the POKE command and read data from it with the PEEK command. Furthermore since it is unlikely that you will have any need to entirely fill the 64K of memory space available in the Sinclair, competition for memory space will not be a serious problem. All the projects in this book will be interfaced as memory.

Data formats

All data in the computer must be handled as binary. Thus when the computer receives the command

LET X = 10

a memory location actually receives the binary number 00001010. But how do you think the computer handles the non-numerical elements of that command? There obviously is no way to express the word LET or an X in binary terms. It gets around this problem by representing each of the alphabetic characters by a one-byte code. Table 1-1 reveals that an A is

---

*$\overline{\text{IOREQ}}$ stands for Input/Output Request. Since a bar is over the mnemonic designator, it is low when the signal is active. These signals provide precise timing for transfer of information onto and off of the data bus and will be explained in detail in future chapters. $\overline{\text{MREQ}}$ is the standard signal designation for Memory Request; the bar over the letters signifies that it is a signal which is low when the signal is active also.

represented by a 38 (decimal), a B by a 39, a C by a 40, and so on. It becomes obvious that I/O devices may either want data in binary form or else they may want these alphanumeric codes, depending on the device. For example, you would want the interface for a joystick to read a binary number, which is proportional to the angle of the stick. On the other hand, you would want to send alphanumeric character codes to a line printer. The two data types are handled separately in BASIC as numeric and string variables. Clearly you must be careful when designing an interface to determine which type of data format you will be working with.

TABLE 1.1: The Sinclair Character Code

CODE	CHARACTER	HEX	CODE	CHARACTER	HEX
11	”	0B	37	9	25
12	£	0C	38	A	26
13	$	0D	39	B	27
14	:	0E	40	C	28
15	?	0F	41	D	29
16	(	10	42	E	2A
17	)	11	43	F	2B
18	>	12	44	G	2C
19	<	13	45	H	2D
20	=	14	46	I	2E
21	+	15	47	J	2F
22	−	16	48	K	30
23	*	17	49	L	31
24	/	18	50	M	32
25	;	19	51	N	33
26	,	1A	52	O	34
27	.	1B	53	P	35
28	0	1C	54	Q	36
29	1	1D	55	R	37
30	2	1E	56	S	38
31	3	1F	57	T	39
32	4	20	58	U	3A
33	5	21	59	V	3B
34	6	22	60	W	3C
35	7	23	61	X	3D
36	8	24	62	Y	3E
			63	Z	3F

Virtually all of the world's computers use a standard code for representing the alphanumeric characters. This code is referred to as the ASCII code (American Standard Code for Information Interchange). Because of this standard there are thousands of peripheral devices available that communicate through this code. Unfortunately Sinclair computers are an exception to this rule. Sinclair's code is quite different from ASCII. This difference can cause special problems if you wish to interface to a device that expects ASCII. There are, however, several solutions to this problem that will be presented in later chapters.

Logic chips

Today's computers are built with integrated circuits. An integrated circuit consists of many transistors, diodes, and resistors all together on one small chip of silicon that makes up a complete electrical circuit. Today's technology permits thousands of individual components to be put on a single chip the size of the head of a pin. What is really amazing is that most of these integrated circuits, or ICs as they are more commonly called, range in cost from pennies to just a few dollars. Over the years, there has been a steady evolution of logic families and packaging in the IC industry. Logic families such as DTL (diode-transistor logic) and RTL (resistor-transistor logic) have come and gone, but in the past decade three basic families have emerged and have dominated the industry. They are TTL (transistor-transistor logic), low-power Schottky, and CMOS (complementary metal-oxide semiconductor). The industry has also adopted a standard nomenclature and packaging system in the 7400 series of logic chips. The numbering system is the same for all three families. Low-power Schottky devices are designated by an ''LS'' following the prefix 74, such as a 74LS02. CMOS is identified by a ''C,'' and TTL devices do not use any identifier. These ICs make perfect building blocks for the experimenter, as most of the logic functions you will require can be found in this series. Furthermore they are readily available in retail electronic outlets—which is a big help. Whenever possible, we will utilize 7400 series chips for the projects in this book.

Logic ins and outs

The Sinclair computer and the 7400 series of ICs both use the same logic system of representing 1 by 2.6 to 5 volts and 0 by 0 to .6 volts. All these chips have basically 2 types of connections—inputs and outputs. An input has a relatively high impedance and senses the level of the voltage applied to it. In contrast, an output has a very low impedance and can supply current in such a way as to keep itself at its required logic state. This arrangement allows the designer to have the output of one IC driving the input of another so that the ICs can communicate with one another in the circuit. In general, an output within any given family can drive 5 or more inputs in the same family before the ability of that output to supply current will be overtaxed. This quality is called *fan out*. Although an output line may be tied to many inputs, it should almost never be tied to another output as there will be conflict about the resulting level if the two outputs disagree in their respective logic states. Such a test of wills will certainly result in ambiguous logic states and, with some chips, such as high-power buffers, can even result in rather spectacular burnouts. There are 2 special exceptions to this rule. The first is the *open-collector* device, which may have multiple outputs tied together. Open-collector devices can only pull down the voltage to 0 and are incapable of pulling it up to +5. Thus open-collector outputs must be pulled up to +5 volts by an external "pull-up" resistor to the system power. If any 1 of the outputs on that line goes to an active low, the entire line will be pulled down. In general, we will not be concerned with open-collector devices in this book, but you should be aware of them in your circuit design so that you do not try to use one of them as if it were a normal logic chip. The second exception is the family of 3-state devices; these devices can have their outputs tied together as long as only 1 device is active at a time.

The differences between the 3 logic families lie primarily in their input and output impedances. TTL, the oldest logic family, has a relatively low input impedance in the thousands of ohms. TTL outputs will supply considerable power. TTL devices are cheap but they require a great deal of power-supply current and thus generate a lot of heat. Low-power Schottky devices use about one-fifth the power of TTL and have about 5–10 times the input impedance of the TTL devices. CMOS, which is basically constructed out of field-effect transistors, has input impedances in the megohms and draws miniscule amounts of power. In general, we will concentrate on the low-power Schottky family in this book. We chose that family because the Sinclair outputs are capable of driving several LS loads safely. We have found that many of the Sinclair's outputs will be overloaded with even one TTL load applied to them. In general, CMOS chips can be substituted in any of the projects that specify a low-power Schottky device. We have avoided them simply because CMOS chips are relatively new and can be hard to locate unless you happen to live in a large city.

Logic functions

Digital logic is not difficult to understand, and Sinclair computer users should be familiar with the basic AND and OR functions. The following truth table shows a simple AND function:

IN 1	IN 2	OUT
0	0	0
0	1	0
1	0	0
1	1	1

Note that a 1 will occur in the output only if both inputs are in a high state: IN 1 and IN 2. Contrast this to the OR function below:

IN 1	IN 2	OUT
0	0	0
0	1	1
1	0	1
1	1	1

In this case, the output will be a 1 if either IN 1 or IN 2 is high. Note that for the 0 condition, the OR gate serves an AND function. That is, a 0 output will occur only if IN 1 is 0 and IN 2 is 0. What is the 0 logic function of the AND gate?

If the output of the gate is complemented (inverted), we put an N in front of the name. Thus the truth table for a NAND gate would be:

IN 1	IN 2	OUT
0	0	1
0	1	1
1	0	1
1	1	0

Similarly for a NOR gate, the truth table would be as follows:

IN 1	IN 2	OUT
0	0	1
0	1	0
1	0	0
1	1	0

FIGURE 1-2
Logic symbols.

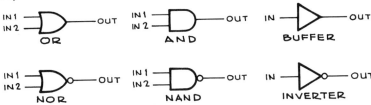

The AND and the OR functions are represented by special symbols, as shown in Figure 1-2. Note that the NOR or complement form is indicated by an open circle on the lead which is complemented. The triangular symbols to the right of the figure show buffers and inverters. The buffers are useful in amplifying a signal so that it may fan out to more inputs. The complement form is useful when the signal must be inverted. Figure 1-3 shows the pin configuration of the 74LS00 Quad NAND gate, the 74LS02 Quad NOR gate, and the 74LS04 hex buffer. Vcc refers to the +5 volt power connection, and GND is, of course, the system ground.

Finally all of the 7400 series ICs come in the familiar DIP (dual-inline

FIGURE 1-3
Common gates: the 74LS00, 74LS02, and 74LS04.
Courtesy Motorola Semiconductor Products, Inc.

74LS00

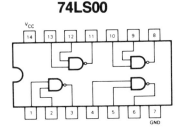

74LS02

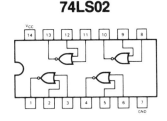

74LS04

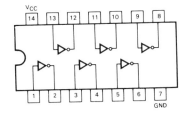

11

package) package. Figure 1-4 shows that when the chip is viewed from the top (with the pins pointing away from you) and the Pin 1 indicator is up, Pin 1 will be to the top left. The pin numbers are then in sequence going counterclockwise around the chip. There may be from 4 to 40 pins on the chip, but they will all use this convention for pin numbering.

FIGURE 1-4
Pin numbering conventions for ICs
using the dual-inline package

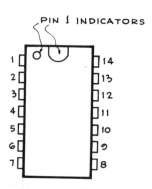

INTEGRATED CIRCUIT WITH PINS
POINTING AWAY FROM VIEWER.

2

CONSTRUCTION TECHNIQUES

Over the years, many different techniques for building custom circuits have been tried; the beginning experimenter can become quite confused by the numerous breadboard and Kluge kits available. In our opinion, wire wrap is by far the most suitable construction technique for building the projects in this book. Wire-wrap tools and parts are easily obtained at almost any retail electronics store, and they are inexpensive. Because no soldering is involved, the projects can be disassembled after they are no longer needed and the parts recovered for future use. Yet when wire-wrap projects are completed, they are neat looking and the connections are reliable. The same techniques have been used in million-dollar computer systems for years.

Wire-wrap construction

Wire-wrap projects are built on phenolic perfboard with holes spaced 0.1″ apart. The 0.1″ spacing is critical as it will accommodate integrated circuit sockets perfectly. Other spacings that are available will not. We have used the Vector brand 3719-4 board for the projects in this book and recommend it highly. Its dimensions are 9.6″ × 4.5″, and it has a 72-position edge connector with 0.1″ spacing on one end. The advantage of the edge connector is that it has the same spacing as the Sinclair's expansion connector and thus you can reconstruct the expansion bus so that the 16K RAM Pack or the printer can still be used when your interface is attached to the computer. This board is available from Jameco Electronics, 1021 Howard Street, San Carlos, California 94070 and Priority One Electronics, 9161 Deering Avenue, Chatsworth, California 91311. Figure 2-1 shows how to modify the connector on the board so that it will accept Sinclair peripherals. The perfboard cuts easily with a hacksaw or a nibbler.

Integrated circuits are mounted on the board by placing them in wire-wrap integrated-circuit sockets. The pins of the sockets are pushed through the holes so that the base of the socket sits flush with the board. Wire wraps on the socket's pins will hold the sockets in place, but they will be wobbly. If you are building a permanent project, you should consider fastening the sockets to the board. It is done with a drop of epoxy glue under each socket.

Many components such as capacitors and resistors do not have wire-wrap leads. These components can be accommodated by using VECTOR T44 push-in terminals. T44 terminals mechanically fit tightly in the perfboard holes and have solder terminals on top of the board and wire-wrap tails below it. These terminals are also useful in making wire-wrap connections to the printed circuit (PC) plug at the end of the board as they can be soldered directly to the foil bands.

FIGURE 2-1
Modifying the connector on the VECTOR board so that the Sinclair expansion connector is duplicated. Cut the phenolic as shown with a hacksaw or a nibbler.

FIGURE 2-2
Photos of a partially completed board. The **a** panel
shows ICs in wire-wrap sockets and components
soldered to Vector® T44 terminals. The **b** panel
shows the bottom of the board with the wire-wraps.

a

b

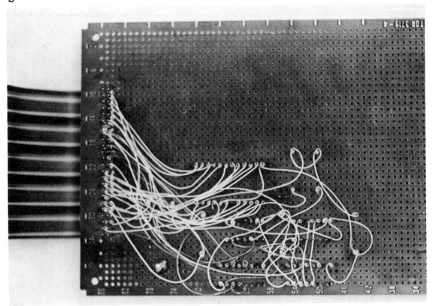

Connectors for the Sinclair

As of this writing, we are unable to locate a supplier for a plug compatible with the expansion connector on the Sinclair computer. To overcome this problem we have resorted to cutting down a 50-pin-card edge connector with a hacksaw. We used an AP Products 0.1″ spacing 50-contact connector with 36″ of 50-conductor ribbon cable molded into the plug (available from Priority One Electronics, order number 05924066-36). We cut out one contact on either end of the plug with the hacksaw and filed the edges smooth. You should use the expansion slot in the Sinclair's case to guide you in cutting the connector in the right place. A small scrap of plastic can be glued into position 3 for a key. If the connector is carefully cut to fit the hole in the case it will automatically align itself; as a result we have found the key to be unnecessary.

The 46 wires in the ribbon cable can be soldered to T44 terminals pressed into the board. That is a tedious procedure, however, and it is difficult to avoid shorts. A much more efficient way to mate to the expansion board is to put a 50-pin socket connector on the other end of the

FIGURE 2-3
Cutting the edge-connector socket. A 25-pin socket is cut in the center of the first and the 25th contact to make the 23-pin connector required for the Sinclair. Photo on p. 17 shows the completed connector.

ribbon cable. This socket connector has a double row of receptacles spaced 0.1″ apart that accept the .025″ square wire-wrap posts. This socket is designed to be pressed onto the ribbon cable by squeezing the assembly together in a vise. We used the Winchester 25/50 socket connector from Priority One Electronics (order number 051DC50SKT). It then mates with a wire-wrap header that sits on the expansion board like an IC socket. We used the Winchester straight wire-wrap 25/50 gold header from Priority One Electronics (order number 051DCSTH50WW). You can then pick off the required signals from the wire-wrap pins at the base of the header. Figure 2-4 shows the entire assembly as described above. Remember that the 2 pins on each end of the header have no connections and should be ignored.

Pin assignments on the expansion connector

Figure 2-5 shows the pin assignments on the edge connector in the back of your Sinclair computer. The figure shows a rear view of the computer. Pin 3 is the keyway and has no signal assigned to it. The ZX80, ZX81 and Timex 1000 all have identical signal assignments with the exception of the ROMCS (read-only memory chip select). This signal is absent from the ZX80 models. It is very easy to make mistakes in locating the proper signal at the ribbon cable's termination on the expansion board. We strongly suggest that you double check the pin assignments by placing an ohm meter between the Sinclair's edge connector and the wire-wrap pins on the

17

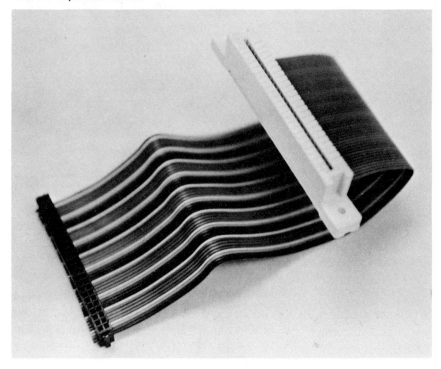

expansion board. Once verified, the pins should be clearly labeled with a marking pencil to avoid any future wiring errors.

Building a logic probe

An invaluable tool for troubleshooting digital circuits is the logic probe. If you are going to execute one or more of the projects in this book, we urge you to either buy one or build the logic probe described here. A logic probe consists of three light emitting diode (LED) indicators. When the probe is placed on a line, the indicators HIGH, LOW, or PULSE light when the line is in a logic high, a logic low, or a transition from one state to another, respectively. The logic probe has replaced the multimeter as the basic electronics tool for the digital troubleshooter.

Figure 2-6 shows the schematic of a logic probe. It can be easily built on a $2'' \times 4''$ piece of perfboard. Wire-wrap construction, as described on pages 13 and 14, should be used. Attach a $12''$ piece of 22-gauge insulated wire with a small alligator clip on the Vcc and GND pins. Use a red wire for

FIGURE 2-5
Signals on the Sinclair edge connector (as viewed from
the back of the computer)

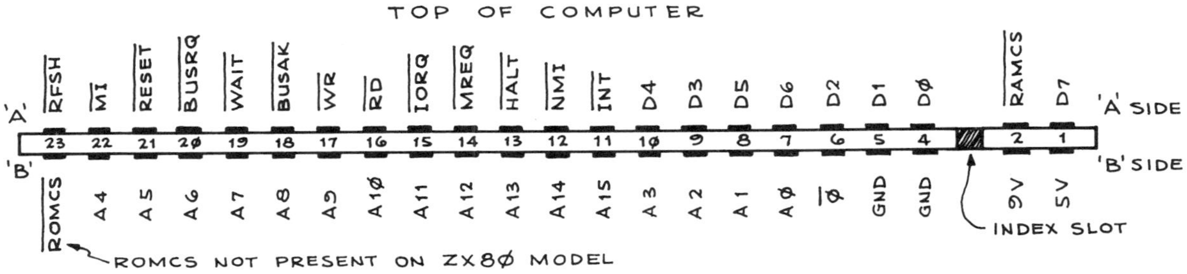

TOP OF COMPUTER

'A' SIDE

'B' SIDE

INDEX SLOT

ROMCS NOT PRESENT ON ZX8Ø MODEL

'A' side	Pin	'B' side
D7	1	5V
RAMCS	2	9V
D0	4	GND
D1	5	GND
D2	6	Ø
D6	7	Ø A
D5	8	A1
D3	9	A2
D4	10	A3
INT	11	A15
NMI	12	A14
HALT	13	A13
MREQ	14	A12
IORQ	15	A11
RD	16	A1Ø
WR	17	A9
BUSAK	18	A8
WAIT	19	A7
BUSRQ	20	A6
RESET	21	A5
M1	22	A4
RFSH	23	ROMCS

FIGURE 2-6

Logic probe schematic. This simple logic probe is an invaluable tool for testing digital circuits.

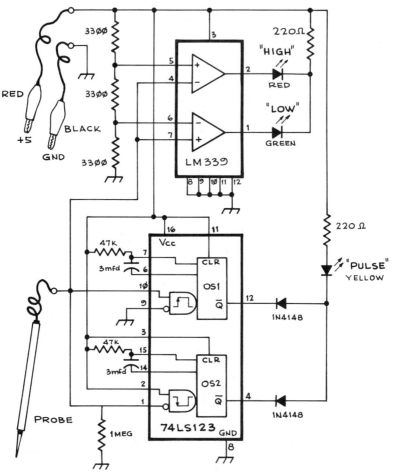

Vcc and a black one for GND. These wires are used to pick up power from the system under test. A third 12″ wire should be used for the test lead and should terminate in a pointed probe like the one used on a voltmeter. After the circuit is completed, attach the power leads to a +5 volt source. None of the lights should be on. Touch the probe to Vcc; you should see the HIGH lamp go on. Now touch the probe to GND. The LOW lamp should light, and the PULSE lamp should flash momentarily, indicating that a state change has occurred. The PULSE lamp should flash on either a high-to-low or a low-to-high transition. If no LEDs light, check to see if the LEDs have been inserted backward; also check the polarity of the electrolytic capacitors and look for missing wires in your wire-wrap connections.

FIGURE 2-7
Logic probe photo. The top probe is a commercial unit, while the bottom probe is one built from the schematic in Figure 2-6. Both work well. Top photo reprinted by permission of Heath Company. Copyright © 1978.

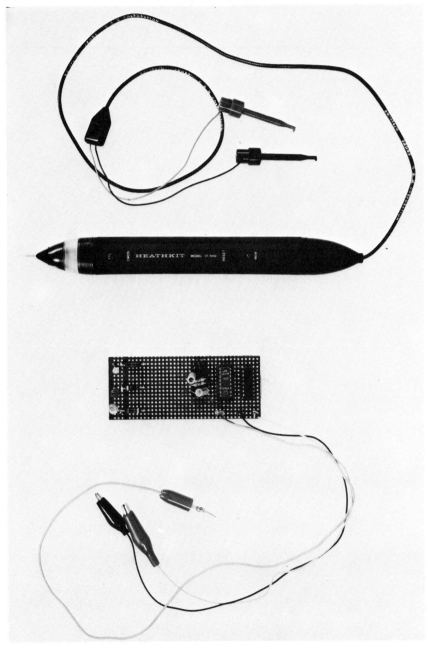

3

CREATING SPACE
FOR EXPANSION
IN THE SINCLAIR

As a Sinclair computer user, you are aware that the Z80 microprocessor is capable of handling 65,536 address units (64K). Your Sinclair computer works in a manner such that its 1K or 2K bytes of RAM occupy one-half of this address space, and the 4K or 8K ROM occupies the other half. This chapter explains what addressing is all about and gives a design for a basic expansion board that circumvents this addressing problem. RAM, ROM and various peripheral devices can later be added to this expansion board.

Fundamentals of addressing

The Z80 microprocessor has a group of 16 pins called address pins A0 through A15. Wires connected from these pins to other devices are called the *address bus*. The Z80, under instructions from the program it is running, activates memory and peripheral devices by putting a combination of high and low voltages on these wires. A unique address, corresponding to 1 memory location or 1 device, might be written as

    LHLLLLLLLLLLHHHHH

where L represents the low voltage (less than 0.6 volts) and H the high voltage (more than 2.6 volts) and the left-most character is the voltage on the highest-subscript address wire, A15. Such a system for representing a unique address would be very unwieldy and difficult to use in written and oral communication and would be subject to errors. In several steps, we'll show how a "shorthand" system can be developed.

First convert all the L values to 0s and all the H values to 1s, like this:

0100000000011111

Since this is a number consisting of all 1s and 0s, we call it a binary number. But we still do not have a suitable shorthand system.

Let's develop a table of the first 16 binary numbers, together with their equivalent decimal numbers and a single-digit arbitrary character to represent the value. Since we anticipate running out of single digits at the number 9, we will continue by using letters of the alphabet:

Decimal Order	Binary Number	Single-Character Representation
0	0000	0
1	0001	1
2	0010	2
3	0011	3
4	0100	4
5	0101	5
6	0110	6
7	0111	7
8	1000	8
9	1001	9
10	1010	A
11	1011	B
12	1100	C
13	1101	D
14	1110	E
15	1111	F

Now if we separate our long binary number into groups of 4 digits each, we have

0100   0000   0001   1111.

If we look up each group in the table and find its corresponding single-character representation, we have the number

401F

which can be written quickly and, more importantly, can be communicated with much less chance of error than the old L/H or 0/1 notation.

Likewise groups of 8 wires having a combination of high and low voltages, such as the contents of a *byte* of memory, can be represented by 2 of our characters; for example,

> LLHHHLHL
> or 0 0 1 1 1 0 1 0

can be represented as 3A in our new notation.

This single-character system of representing a group of 4 highs and lows (4 *bits* of information) is the hexadecimal notation commonly used to describe computer operations. Its name comes from the 16 characters (0–F) used as its set of digits. In our everyday number system we use 10 characters (0–9). A decimal number such as 6789 means to us

>   9 1s
> plus 8 10s
> plus 7 100s
> plus 6 1,000s

Moving 1 digit to the left increases its "weight" by tenfold. Our hexadecimal, or hex, number has a similar weighting of each digit, although the weighting is by a factor of 16 rather than 10. Each digit has a weight 16 times the weight of the digit to its right.

With this information, we can convert our hex number $401F to a number in our familiar decimal notation (from now on we will distinguish hex numbers by the dollar sign):

> $F 15 1s   =   15
> $1   1 16s   =   16
> $0   0 256s =   0
> $4   4 4096s = 16384
>   total   16415

You will need to use this conversion of a hex number to decimal in your projects; while addresses are more easily understood in the hex notation, Sinclair's BASIC language must be given numbers in decimal. Some BASICs support hex numbers, and it is ironic that Sinclair's BASIC reconverts decimal numbers to hex before it uses them.

Decoding

Your Z80 microprocessor selects one of 65,536 addresses ($0000 through $FFFF) by placing the address's highs and lows on the Z80 address bus. *Decoding* is the process of generating an electrical signal, or *strobe*, whenever a particular address combination appears on the address bus. Decoding may be accomplished by simple logic gates, by decoder chips designed specifically for the purpose, by a chip that serves another purpose (such as RAM or ROM), or by a combination of these. When decoding for memory, a large number of address combinations must be decoded to provide a strobe that activates the memory chip whenever any address in that range is on the bus. Inside the memory chip is another stage of decoding that selects which byte in the range of addresses is to be read. This latter stage of decoding in an 8K ROM, for example, determines which of the 8,192 bytes in the ROM is to be sent to the Z80. In order to make this selection, the lower 13 address lines must be wired directly to the ROM, and the address strobe, decoded from the remaining 3 address lines, is wired to the ROM's chip-select pin. The chip select requires a low in order for the ROM to become active.

In a fully decoded system, all of the upper 3 address lines—A13, A14, and A15—would be wired to a decoder that would provide a low-going strobe to select the ROM when its address range (for example, $0000–1FFF) is selected. As a cost compromise, most computers do not fully decode addresses, and this is true of Sinclair computers. In the ZX80 and ZX81, the 4K or 8K ROM is activated when address line A14 is at a low level, and the 1K or 2K RAM is active when A14 is at a high level.

What does this do to the address space? Let's look at our 16 address wires for an 8K ROM and analyze the situation:

X0XA-AAAA-AAAA-AAAA

The 0 represents A14 at a low level, the As are on-chip decoding, and the Xs mean the wire is not connected. The program in the ROM is written to run at addresses $0000–$1FFF. Certainly the ROM will respond in this range, since if the Xs are replaced by 0s this will be a proper address range. But there are 3 other combinations of values for the two Xs that also activate the ROM—0 and 1, 1 and 0, and 1 and 1. This means that the ROM will also be activated whenever 3 other 8K blocks are addressed; that is, there will be 3 "images" of the ROM in the Sinclair's 64K universe at addresses

$2000-$3FFF
$8000-$9FFF
$A000-$BFFF

The situation is similar with 4K ROMs, except that there are 7 4K images. Both the 4K and 8K ROMs are said to *occupy* 32K of address space due to incomplete decoding.

The 1K or 2K RAM, similarly, occupies 32K of address space, with 31 or 15 images.

There went our entire 64K! But don't despair. The clever Sinclair designers provided a means of disabling the decoding on the Sinclair board and permit decoding on an external board.

Here is a BASIC program you can run to prove the existence of the images described above:

PROGRAM	COMMENTS
10 LET START = 0	ROM starts at 0
20 LET B = PEEK (START)	Look at first byte
30 FAST	Omit for ZX80
40 FOR A = 0 to 65535 STEP 1024	
50 IF PEEK A = B THEN PRINT A,	
60 NEXT A	
70 SLOW	Omit for ZX80

The program places the contents of the first byte of the ROM into B. The loop in lines 40–60 compares B with the first byte in every 1K block and prints the address only if it matches. For the ZX81 or Timex, the screen should show:

0	8192
32768	40960

This display indicates that the ROM repeated itself 4 times in the Sinclair's memory space. For the ZX80, which has only a 4K ROM, the screen will look like this:

0	4096
8192	12288
32768	36864
40960	45056

Note that the 4K ROM repeats itself 8 times in the memory space. The program can be modified to test the RAM by changing line 10 to:

10 LET START = 16384

The remainder of this chapter will be devoted to the design of a basic expansion board with power supply and sufficient decoding to free up memory space for your desired peripherals, which may be:

Expansion RAM
Expansion ROM
Parallel input/output
Serial input/output
Analog devices

The expansion board and connectors

The basic expansion board is required for the addition of any major circuit shown in this book. We do not envision that all the projects be placed on an expansion board at one time; in fact, it is probably impossible to add all the circuitry without buffering the address, data, and control lines. We added 1 or 2 projects at a time, tested them, and then rewired the board for other projects.

Because of the ease of construction and later modification, we have used standard wire-wrap techniques. We discourage the use of the new wire-wrap models that do not require stripping. They have the disadvantage of unreliable connections, and they are difficult to modify for later projects. Details of board-wiring techniques are given in Chapter 2.

The power supply

While most of our projects could be powered from the Sinclair's 5-volt regulated supply, we recommend adding the 5-volt regulator circuit shown in Figure 3-1 in order to avoid generating additional heat inside the Sinclair computer's case. The 7805 regulator is recommended and should be on a heat sink. Its output should be bypassed to ground by a Tantalum capacitor. It requires 9 volts from the Sinclair's power transformer.

After the power supply is built, measure the resistance between the 9-volt connection and ground, as well as the resistance between the 5-volt regulated output connection and ground. If either of these indicates a dead short, *do not power up the board*. Check your wiring. If necessary,

FIGURE 3-1
5-volt regulator circuit. It reduces 9 volts to 5 volts for
use on the expansion board.

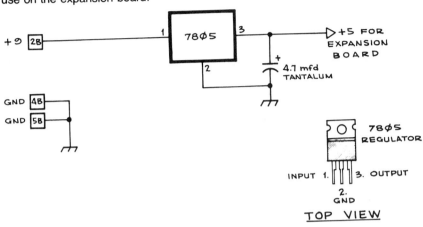

disconnect the capacitor and/or regulator to help isolate the problem.
Replace the problem component.

If all appears well, plug in the expansion board and power up. The
voltage on the regulator output should be 5 volts ± 0.25.

The ROM decoder

It is said that there are as many ways to decode as there are designers. We
have elected to utilize the 74LS138 3-line to 8-line decoder, which has 3
gates for additional control. It is a low-power Schottky device, which
means that its loading on the Sinclair expansion bus will be about one-fifth
that of a standard TTL device. The purpose of our ROM decoder is to take
over the decoding of the Sinclair ROM from the minimum on-board
decoder and activate the ROM only when its primary addresses are active,
thereby eliminating the ROM images. The space now made available can
be used by any device we desire.

The Sinclair designers had such an arrangement in mind on the ZX81;
if you are brave enough to make a minor modification to your ZX80 board,
it can also use the ROM decoder. The ZX81 circuitry simply has a 680-ohm
resistor between the decoder and the ROM, which you can overwhelm by
trying the ROMCS' line to 5 volts via a 270-ohm resistor on the expansion
board.

If yours is the ZX80, you should make the modification to your
printed circuit board shown in Figure 3-2 to allow the external decoder to

FIGURE 3-2
Modifying the ZX80 circuit board for use with the ROM decoder. (a) The panel on this page is a schematic of the changes. (b) The panel on the opposite page shows the 600 Ω resistor (arrow) across the severed trace on the ZX80 board. Don't forget the wire to Pin 23 of the expansion connector.

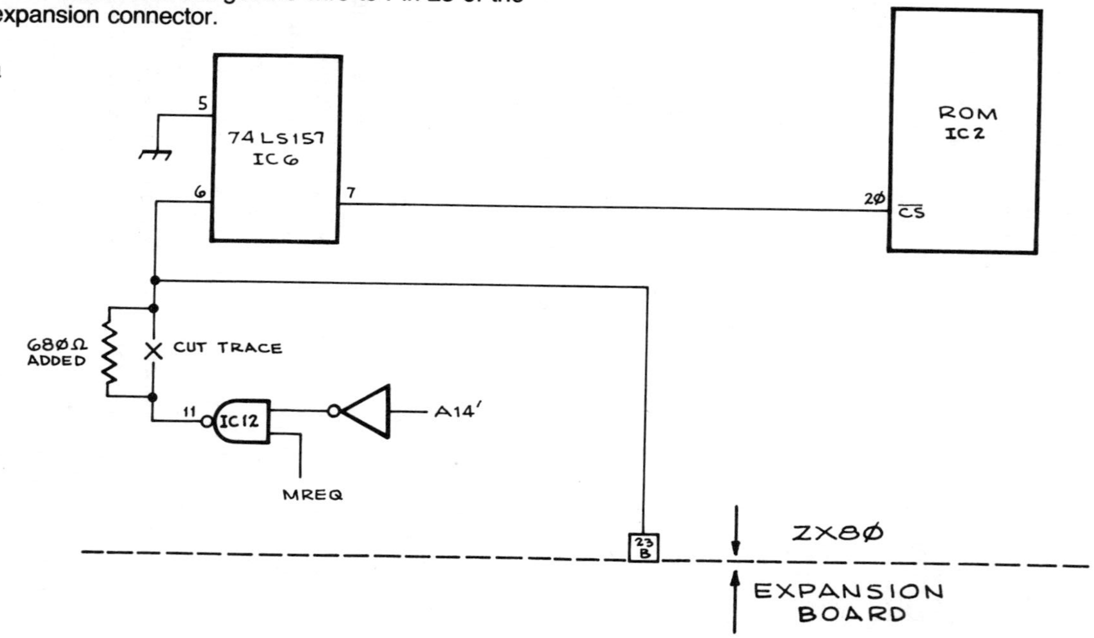

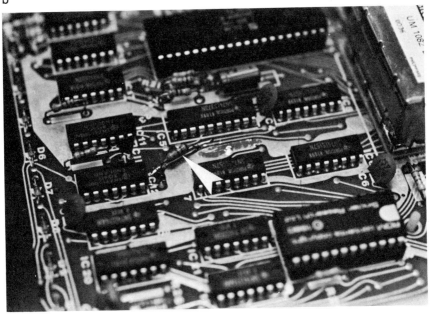

work. You must cut the trace as shown and solder a 680-ohm resistor across the cut. Add a jumper wire from the end of the resistor farthest from the keyboard to position 23-bottom (opposite end from the key slot) of the expansion connector.

The ROM decoder for 8K ROMs is shown in Figure 3-3. It will also work for 4K ROMs; we recommend that it be used as is for 4K ROMs, in case you wish to later upgrade to 8K. To understand its operation, refer to the truth table for the 74LS138 shown in Figure 3-4. The 8 outputs are active low, and only 1 may go low at a time, as selected by the A, B, and C inputs. Unless G1 is high and both G2A and G2B are low, no output will go low. G2B is tied to active-low $\overline{MREQ}$ from the expansion connector, so that the decoder will be active only during the Z80's memory request time. G2A is connected to A15, while G1 receives A14 via an inverter (74LS04). We have therefore, the following situation on the address bus when decoding occurs:

A15	A14	A13	A12	A11	A10–A0
0	0	C	B	A	X

31

FIGURE 3-3

Schematic of the ROM decoder. Circuit is used to free
up address space formerly occupied by ROM images.

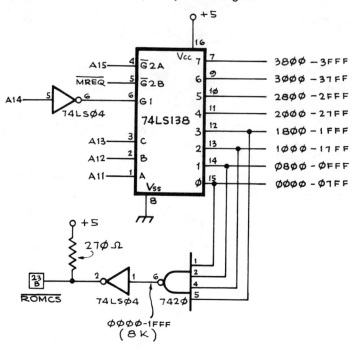

The outputs will have the following address ranges:

INPUTS			OUTPUT
C	B	A	ADDRESS RANGE
0	0	0	$0000–$07FF
0	0	1	$0800–$0FFF
0	1	0	$1000–$17FF
0	1	1	$1800–$1FFF
1	0	0	$2000–$27FF
1	0	1	$2800–$2FFF
1	1	0	$3000–$37FF
1	1	1	$3800–$3FFF

We have thus broken down a 16K address space into 8 2K blocks. The
74LS20 combines 4 of these to decode the exact address requirement for an
8K ROM at $0000–$1FFF, and this signal is passed back to the main
computer via an inverter gate (1/6 74LS04). Note also that the ROM will no

32

FIGURE 3-4

Data for the 74LS138 and 74LS20. The 74LS138 is a fast, low-power decoder providing eight outputs from three binary input lines. Courtesy Motorola Semiconductor Products, Inc.

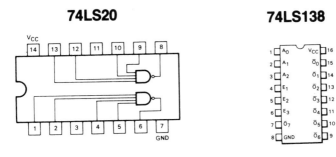

74LS20   74LS138

74LS138
TRUTH TABLE

INPUTS						OUTPUTS							
$\bar{E}_1$	$\bar{E}_2$	E_3	A_0	A_1	A_2	$\bar{O}_0$	$\bar{O}_1$	$\bar{O}_2$	$\bar{O}_3$	$\bar{O}_4$	$\bar{O}_5$	$\bar{O}_6$	$\bar{O}_7$
H	X	X	X	X	X	H	H	H	H	H	H	H	H
X	H	X	X	X	X	H	H	H	H	H	H	H	H
X	X	L	X	X	X	H	H	H	H	H	H	H	H
L	L	H	L	L	L	L	H	H	H	H	H	H	H
L	L	H	H	L	L	H	L	H	H	H	H	H	H
L	L	H	L	H	L	H	H	L	H	H	H	H	H
L	L	H	H	H	L	H	H	H	L	H	H	H	H
L	L	H	L	L	H	H	H	H	H	L	H	H	H
L	L	H	H	L	H	H	H	H	H	H	L	H	H
L	L	H	L	H	H	H	H	H	H	H	H	L	H
L	L	H	H	H	H	H	H	H	H	H	H	H	L

H = HIGH Voltage Level
L = LOW Voltage Level
X = Don't Care

longer respond to its images at $8000–$9FFF and $A000–$BFFF. The remaining 4 2K blocks will be used in our expansion projects.

To build the ROM decoder, you will need a 16-pin socket for the 74LS138 and 2 14-pin sockets for the 74LS04 and 74LS20. Glue the sockets to the board, taking care that glue does not get on the wire-wrap pins. Wire according to Figure 3-3 and don't forget the power and ground pins. Again, check the resistance between the 5-volt bus and ground before applying power; *do not proceed* with a dead short.

If all appears well, connect to the Sinclair, power up, and make sure the Sinclair is working. If not, recheck your wiring and your cable continuity. You may rerun the program presented earlier and verify the operation. Proper decoding will result in a single 0 on the screen, with no images. The following program can also be used as verification:

```
10 FOR I = 8180 TO 8200
20 SCROLL
30 PRINT I, PEEK I
40 NEXT I
```

This program will print the last portion of the ROM through address 8181 ($1FFF). At address 8192 and beyond, the PEEKs should all be 255, indicating the ROM is not enabled at these addresses.

You may also wish to disconnect the expansion board (power off first) and rerun this program to see the images begin at 8192.

The new memory map

With the ROM fully decoded, we are now in a position to use memory space formerly occupied by ROM images to locate other devices, such as protected RAM, expansion ROM, serial or parallel I/O devices, and so on. A few of these possibilities are covered in succeeding chapters. We have 4 unused 2K address strobes that can be used directly to activate devices, or they can be further broken down into a number of narrower-range strobes for many more useful strobes.

The reset button

The Sinclair computer resets the Z80 each time the power is turned on. You will not have used your Sinclair very long before you will have encountered a *system crash*. In a system crash the Z80 microprocessor literally gets lost—the screen goes blank or fills with garbage. The keys become ineffective or do strange things. A common cause of a system crash is a read error when loading from cassette, but other things may cause it as well. When it happens your only recourse is to cycle the power and restart the system. Unfortunately, in Sinclair's zeal for economy, they did not include a power switch. Therefore you must unplug the power cord and fumble with the plug until you find the hole in which to reinsert it. This inconvenience can be eliminated by including a reset button on your interface board. The reset button should be a single-pole, normally open, momentary-contact switch. Wire one side of the switch to ground and the other side to the $\overline{\text{RESET}}$ line—Pin 21A on the Sinclair's connector. Each time the button is pressed, the memory will be cleared and the system restarted.

FIGURE 3-5
Memory maps. *Left:* the original map showing memory
images. *Right:* revised map obtained by further
decoding of address space.

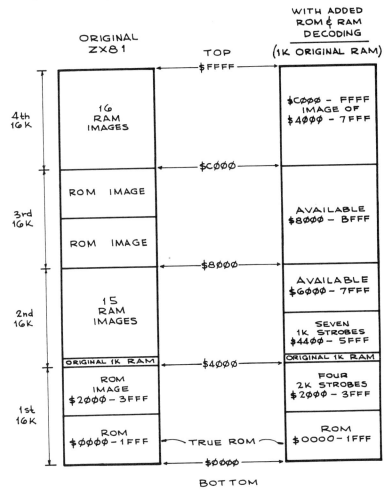

WITH ADDED
ROM & RAM
DECODING

ORIGINAL
ZX81

TOP

(1K ORIGINAL RAM)

$FFFF

4th
16K

16
RAM
IMAGES

$C000 – FFFF
IMAGE OF
$4000 – 7FFF

$C000

3rd
16K

ROM   IMAGE

ROM   IMAGE

AVAILABLE
$8000 – BFFF

$8000

2nd
16K

15
RAM
IMAGES

AVAILABLE
$6000 – 7FFF

SEVEN
1K STROBES
$4400 – 5FFF

ORIGINAL 1K RAM

$4000

ORIGINAL 1K RAM

1st
16K

ROM
IMAGE
$2000 – 3FFF

FOUR
2K STROBES
$2000 – 3FFF

ROM
$0000 – 1FFF

TRUE ROM

ROM
$0000 – 1FFF

$0000

BOTTOM

Damage to the Sinclair

Our experience with the Sinclair has been that it is extremely tolerant of
shorts on the expansion connector and that errors in wiring your projects
usually will not result in any permanent damage to the computer itself.
Certain combinations of errors, however, could potentially do permanent

35

damage. Should a dead system result from an unsuccessful "smoke test" with a new project, you might proceed as follows:

1. Is there system power? Check for exactly 5 volts on Pin 11 of the Z80 chip. If it is lower than 4.5 volts or higher than 5.5 volts, check the regulator chip and the power supply itself.

2. Is there a blown chip? If possible, obtain chips from a friend's computer to substitute in the sockets. Try one at a time until the problem is found. Also try your chips in his or her computer to verify that they are all okay. Be sure to turn off the computer before removing or inserting an IC.

3. Is the system clock working? Put a logic probe on Pin 6 of the Z80. It should indicate pulses. If not, check the ceramic filter and transistor Q1.

4

PARALLEL OUTPUT PORTS

In Chapter 3 we demonstrated how to decode memory addresses in your Sinclair computer. We found that a strobe pulse for data transfer between memory and the Z80 processor was generated whenever both the pattern on the 16-line address was true and MREQ went low. If the WRITE line was low at that time, data was to be transferred from the Z80 to memory. If the READ line was low, the transfer was to be in the opposite direction.

I/O devices as memory

Transfers to and from memory are accomplished whenever the Z80 processor executes a memory-reference type of instruction. For example, you can examine or change a memory location's contents with the BASIC commands PEEK and POKE, respectively. These commands simply cause the Z80 to either read the contents of the memory location specified in the PEEK command and return that value to BASIC or to store the value indicated by the POKE command at the specified address.

The Z80 processor is designed to handle input/output (I/O) devices in a similar manner. An I/O transfer strobe is generated by a true pattern on the first 8 address lines A_0–A_7 and by the IOREQ line being low. Just as in the case of a memory transfer, data is leaving the Z80 processor when the

$\overline{\text{WRITE}}$ line is low and data is entering the Z80 when the $\overline{\text{READ}}$ line is low. Since only the first 8 address lines are involved in selecting a device address, 2^8 or 256 devices can be interfaced to the Z80. Transfers between the Z80 and an I/O device occur whenever the Z80 executes an IN or an OUT machine-language instruction. Some microcomputers, such as the Radio Shack TRS-80®, support commands in BASIC called IN or OUT that facilitate communication with I/O devices. Unfortunately Sinclair computers do not offer such commands. This means that external devices interfaced in this manner cannot be easily accessed from BASIC. The solution to this problem is really quite simple, however. You merely interface an external device as though it were memory and effect the communication with the device using the PEEK or POKE commands. This is a perfectly legitimate thing to do. In fact, some microprocessors, such as the 6800 or the 6502, do not even have an I/O port facility, and all devices must be interfaced as memory. The Z80's I/O port architecture was designed so that I/O devices would not compete for true memory space. In Sinclair computers, however, only a small percentage of the Z80's 64K of memory space is filled; thus space is hardly a problem.

I/O device addressing

We also learned in Chapter 3 that although most Sinclair computers are delivered with only 9K or 10K memory, they have no free address space because of incomplete address decoding. To free up some address space so that additional memory or I/O devices could be added, we had to implement some external address decoding on our interface board. This added circuitry created some holes in the memory space to which additions could be made.

Where is the best place to add I/O devices? A glance at the memory map in Figure 3-5 reveals that $4000 to $7FFF (the second 16K block) is reserved for BASIC RAM. Furthermore $C000 to $FFFF (the fourth 16K block) must contain a RAM image. The block $0000 to $1FFF is occupied by the 8K ROM. That leaves 8K of free space between $2000 and $3FFF, the block between the RAM and the ROM. There is also a free space between $8000 and $BFFF (the third 16K block of memory). Since the latter space can be utilized by BASIC by redefining RAM top (the end of BASIC's RAM), we recommend that I/O devices be added in the former space, $2000 to $3FFF. Furthermore, to provide compatibility with the other projects in this book, we suggest that I/O devices only be interfaced in the 2K block between $3000 and $37FF.

The external address decoder for the ROM space is shown in Figure 3-3. Pin 9 of the 74LS138 carries a data-transfer strobe for I/O devices. The 74LS138 octal decoder is active whenever A15 and A14 are both low, the condition which selects the first 16K block of memory. The binary pattern on the 3 address lines A11 through A13 causes 1 of the 8 outputs to be selected and become low. Each output controls a 2K block of memory. The first 4 outputs are used to control the 8K ROM, while the other 4 are available to the user. Thus any PEEK or POKE command between $3000 and $37FF (12288 and 14335 decimal) should cause a data-transfer strobe to appear on Pin 9 of the 74LS138.

The parallel output port

The most common computer interface is the parallel output port. In this configuration, the binary data is carried on 8 separate lines. These lines may, in turn, be connected to an external binary device such as a printer, digital display, card punch, digital to analog converter, and so on. Also each line of the output port may be used separately to open or close a relay, turn on an indicator, or drive some TTL circuit. The possibilities are endless.

The output port requires logic that will capture the data from the 8 data lines at exactly the proper time. The timing diagram in Figure 4-1 shows that when both the data-transfer strobe is low and the WRITE line is low, the binary representation of the data to be output is on the 8 data lines from the Z80 processor. This data can be captured by placing the input of a D flip-flop or a digital latch on each data line and gating it with the output data-transfer strobe. Figure 4-2 shows how the 74LS75 Quad D flip-flop works. When G is high, the output Q follows the input D. When G goes low, however, the Q output stays wherever it was at the time G went low. Thus, as the data transfer strobe goes high, the flip-flops follow the data lines. Since the strobe returns to the low state at the point when the data is stable on the data lines, the 8 flip-flops will hold the data until the next strobe occurs. The digital latch serves the same function but operates on a slightly different principle. Figure 4-2 also shows how the 74LS175 Quad latch works. Whenever the clock input goes from a low to a high state, the outputs assume the states of their inputs at the transition time. The difference is that the outputs never "follow" the data as the D flip-flops do. The result, however, is the same for both devices—data on the input is captured by a critically timed clock pulse. Note that the 74LS75 requires a positive clock pulse while the 74LS175 requires a negative clock pulse. This

FIGURE 4-1
Output timing for the Z80. The data to be output is stable on the data bus when MREQ goes to the high state. One T cycle in the Sinclair computer is about 800ns.

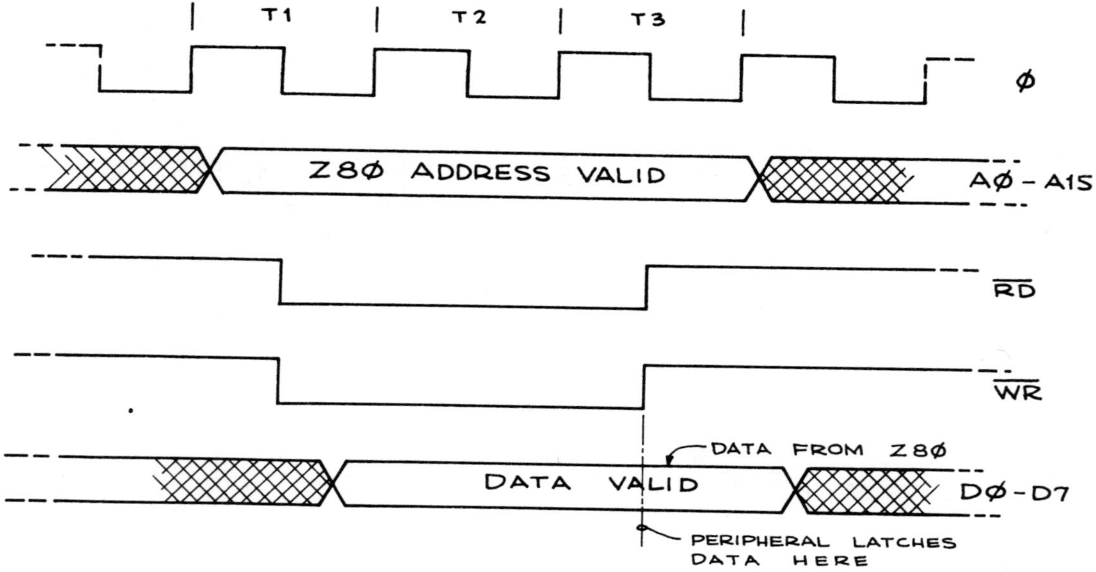

FIGURE 4-2

Digital latches. (a) The left panel shows pin assignments for the 74LS75 and the 74LS175. (b) The right panel shows their operation. Note that the 74LS175 only latches data when the clock goes from a low to a high state. Courtesy Motorola Semiconductor Products, Inc.

a

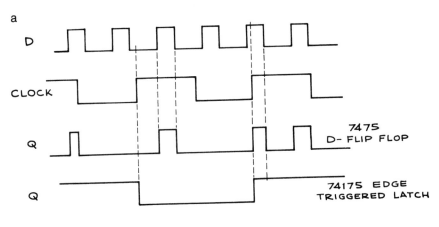

b

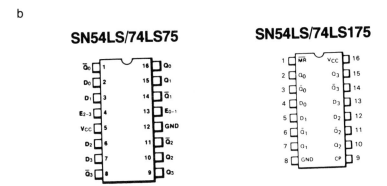

difference can be very important when you are trying to design a circuit with a minimum number of components. Often the choice between these 2 devices will be made on the polarity of the strobe pulse available.

Figure 4-3 shows two 74LS175s used together to latch the data from the data bus. The output is sent to a 16-pin DIP socket, which makes for a convenient connection to the outside world. Also, if you will place eight LEDs in a 16-pin header, as shown in Figure 4-4, you can perform the following exercises, which help illustrate the function of the parallel output port.

FIGURE 4-3
A schematic for the parallel output port

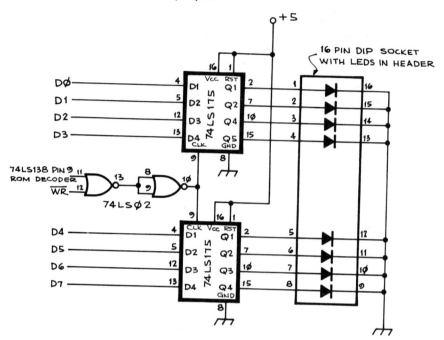

Construction of the parallel output port

This section describes the construction of a general-purpose parallel output port. You should build this port on your interface board especially if you wish to perform the teaching exercise that follows. Make connections as shown in the schematic in Figure 4-3. Double check all connections to make sure that no wiring errors or shorts are present. Although it is not likely, it is possible that your computer could be damaged by certain combinations of miswiring. When you are sure that the board is ready to test, turn off the power and plug the connector into the back of the computer.

Now, with the monitor warmed up, connect the power and see if the cursor appears on the screen. If it does not appear, disconnect the power immediately. You have an error. Check your circuit again and try to locate the problem. If you have verified that the wiring is accurate but the computer still does not operate with the board attached, you may have a bad integrated circuit. Try substituting each IC until the fault is found. Finally make sure that +5 volts is present on the board and that the regulator is functioning normally.

FIGURE 4-4
Photo of LEDs in header plug

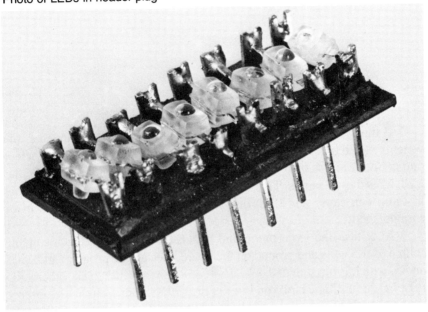

Parallel output port exercises

For this experiment you will need the logic probe described in Chapter 2 and the LED header. With the LED header inserted in the DIP socket, turn on the computer and the monitor. Enter the following program and start it:

```
10 INPUT X
20 POKE 14000,X
30 GOTO 10
```

Responding to the INPUT prompt with a ∅ should cause all of the LEDs to go out. Next enter a 255. This entry should cause all of the LEDs to be lit. If you observe something different, you have a wiring error. If that is the case, locate the problem and correct it before proceeding.

Any LED may be lit by simply outputting the *weight* of its bit. For example, the third LED is on data line 2. Therefore its weight is 2 to the second power, which is 4. Consequently we refer to this line as the 4 weight line. Enter a 4 and observe that only lamp 3 will be lit. The following table shows the weight for each line. Try inputting each of these numbers in the weight column in the program and verify that each will cause the selected LED to light.

OUTPUT LINE	WEIGHT
0	1
1	2
2	4
3	8
4	16
5	32
6	64
7	128

If more than 1 LED is to be lit at once, then merely add together the weights of the bits you wish to select. For example, if you wish to select output lines 2 and 4, then you add a 4 and a 16, which yields 20. Verify that a 20 lights these 2 lamps. Try other combinations until you are comfortable that you can cause any LED or combination of LEDs to become lit or extinguished.

Now take the logic probe and attach the power leads to a suitable source of +5 volts and ground on the board. Restart the program and enter an 85, which is the sum of $1+4+16+64$; it should cause every other LED to be lit. Put the logic probe on Pin 1 of the LED header; you should observe a high state there since this LED is on. Next put the probe on Pin 2. This pin should be low since that LED is off. Verify that all LEDs that you have caused to light have a logic high state and all those that are out have a logic low state. (Note that the voltage to the lit LEDs will not be a full 5 volts since the LEDs will pull the outputs of the 74LS75s down to about 3 volts. This voltage may not be enough to indicate a high state on some logic probes. If the voltage is too low to indicate a high state, you may have to remove the LED header from the socket while making this measurement.)

Next place the probe on Pin 13 of the 74LS02. This pin is the data-transfer strobe. Note that it is low. Now with the probe still attached enter a number into the program. Note that each time a number is entered and the POKE command is executed, a pulse appears on Pin 13 as indicated by a winking of the pulse indicator. Next put the probe on Pin 11. This is the line from the 74LS138 address decoder. Note that it is in a high state with no pulses. Again enter a number into the program and observe that a pulse is generated as this address is selected. Finally put the probe on Pin 12, the WRITE line. Note that the pulse indicator is continuously lit. This line is very busy because the Z80 processor is constantly writing to the keyboard or to RAM as it executes the ROM program. One more write cycle to the output port will not be noticed. Placing the probe on one of the data lines will reveal that these lines are also very busy. That is why it is necessary to LATCH the data as we have done to be able to read it.

An important function of many computer interfaces is to provide critical timing. Such timing can be illustrated by the following program:

```
5 FAST
10 FOR I = 0 TO 7
20 POKE 14000, INT (2**I)
30 PAUSE 30
40 NEXT I
50 GOTO 10
```

This program will cause the LEDs to light in sequence from the first to the last with a change every half second. The PAUSE causes the half-second delay. Prove that by replacing the present line 30 with

```
30 PAUSE 120
```

The change will now occur every 2 seconds.

It should be clear from the foregoing that we now have 8 lines that can either be manipulated independently to control 8 different external devices or used together to carry an 8-bit binary word.

Adding more ports

The parallel output port described here will be found in 2048 sequential locations (12288 to 14335) since only address lines 11 through 15 were decoded by the 74LS138. You can obviously add more ports in this space by decoding the address lines below A11. Figure 4-5 shows how address line 10 can be decoded to split this space in half and create 2 ports. A POKE in the range of $3000 to $33FF will result in A10 being low and thus activate the gate at the top of the figure. Similarly a POKE to addresses from $3400 to $37FF will cause address line 10 to be high and the lower gate to be selected.

A more convenient way to generate more ports is to use another 74LS138. Figure 4-6 shows how the octal decoder breaks the 2K block decoded by Pin 9 of the first 74LS138 into 8 smaller blocks. By connecting WRITE to G_2 of the decoder, you can make each of these outputs an output data-transfer strobe, since a low state on WRITE is included in the selection scheme. Thus the 74LS02 that we used in Figure 4-3 to include WRITE in the strobe would no longer be required.

A word of caution is required at this point for the overly enthusiastic interface builder. The outputs from the Z80 microprocessor will only drive

FIGURE 4-5

Additional decoding for 2 ports. The top strobe will respond to addresses between $3000 and $33FF, the bottom strobe to addresses between $3400 and $37FF. Note how inverters can be used if a negative strobe is required. See Figure 3-3 for the ROM decoder.

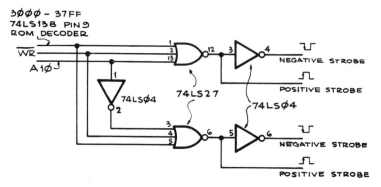

a limited number of integrated circuits. Therefore you should carefully count how many inputs you have tied to each line coming from the computer. In general, each line should be capable of driving at least 3 LS loads. Beyond that you may run into trouble. Excessive loading of the lines

FIGURE 4-6

8 additional strobes. The hex numbers to the right of the figure indicate the addresses to which each pin will respond. The 74LS04 on Pin 15 shows how to generate a positive strobe with an inverter if it is required on any of the signals.

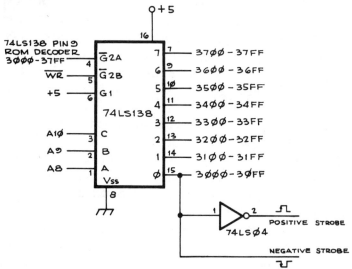

will cause erratic operation of the computer. For multiple output ports loading can easily be remedied by buffering the data lines. Figure 4-7 shows such buffering using 74LS125 3-state buffers. The outputs from these buffers should be capable of driving up to 8 output ports without fear of overloading the data bus. Another problem you should anticipate is that the Sinclair's power supply is quite limited and only a small amount of current can be drawn from it. This problem can be remedied by using a separate power supply for the expansion board. If this separate supply is used, however, be sure to disconnect the connection to the Sinclair's power supply so that the 2 supplies will not interact. Figure 4-9 shows a simple 1-amp supply that will deliver 8 volts of unregulated power supply. Connect the output of this supply to the input of the voltage regulator on the expansion board.

FIGURE 4-7
Buffering the data lines for multiple output ports.
74LS125s are used.

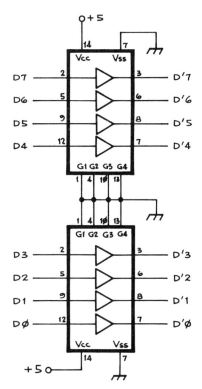

FIGURE 4-8
Data for the 74LS125 and 74LS126. Courtesy Motorola
Semiconductor Products, Inc.

74LS125A

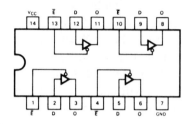

74LS126A

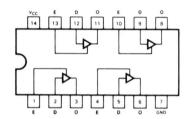

TRUTH TABLES

LS125A		
INPUTS		OUTPUT
$\overline{E}$	D	
L	L	L
L	H	H
H	X	(Z)

LS126A		
INPUTS		OUTPUT
E	D	
H	L	L
H	H	H
L	X	(Z)

L = LOW Voltage Level
H = HIGH Voltage Level
X = Don't Care
(Z) = High Impedance (off)

Controlling high-power devices

The parallel output port just described provides outputs that switch between
0 and +5 volts. The low-power Schottky outputs can only provide a few
milliamps of current and, thus, are very limited in what they can drive. A
very common application for a parallel output port is for each bit of the port
to control a single function; for example, one bit can turn on the coffee pot,
while another bit turns off the living room lights. This delegation of duties
obviously cannot be done with the digital outputs from the LS latches. We
have therefore provided the following series of simple interface circuits
that will help solve such problems.

FIGURE 4-9

An 8-volt unregulated power supply. It can be used if the expansion-board circuit draws more current than the Sinclair's power supply can handle. If this supply is used, connect it to the regulator on the expansion board and remove the connection to the Sinclair's 9-volt supply. CAUTION: The 110-volt section of this circuit is extremely dangerous. Be sure all 110-volt wires are properly insulated.

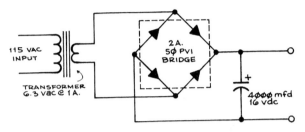

DC loads

Figure 4-10 shows how a simple NPN transistor can be used to switch DC loads on and off under computer control. When the LS output is high, the base of the transistor conducts and allows collector current to pass to the emitter. The 2N4401 will allow up to half an amp of current and will tolerate supply voltages of up to 40 volts DC. If the load is inductive—as in a motor, a solenoid, or the coil of a relay—then you must add the diode around the load so that voltage spikes, which are generated when the device is abruptly turned off, do not destroy the transistor.

FIGURE 4-10

One-half ampere power driver. 1 output bit can control DC loads of up to one-half ampere and 40 volts with this circuit.

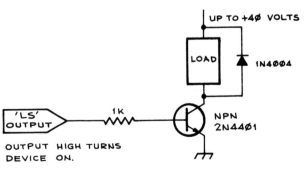

To control a larger load or higher voltages, you will have to use a Darlington driver circuit, as shown in Figure 4-11. The TIP 110 can handle currents of up to 1 full ampere and voltages of up to 60 volts.

AC loads

Many of the devices we wish to control operate on 110-volt house current. Because of the high voltages involved and the high current capability of household 110-volt lines, you must be very careful interfacing such devices to your computer. One inadvertent short and you could reduce your whole computer to a worthless cinder. Therefore, you want to choose devices that will yield reliable isolation between your computer and the power line. Traditionally this precaution has been achieved with relays. There are several relays on the market that can be driven directly by the +5 volts from a latch. Figure 4-12 shows one such relay in use. These relays come in a variety of specifications and can be used for any switching application, including controlling 110 VAC devices of up to 100 to 200 watts.

> CAUTION: Unlike the low voltages found on the logic boards, the 110-volt lines are extremely dangerous. Before plugging these circuits into an outlet, be sure that they are correctly wired, that all connections are properly insulated so that no bare wires exist, and that everything is mechanically secured. DO NOT TOUCH ANY COMPONENTS IN A LIVE 110-VOLT CIRCUIT. Painful shock or even electrocution could result. Also do not connect any device exceeding the power rating of the relay or triac to the controller. The resulting damage may not be limited to the controller.

FIGURE 4-11
1-ampere power driver. This circuit will control DC loads
of up to 1 ampere and 60 volts.

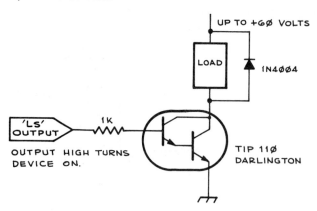

FIGURE 4-12
FIGURE 4-12
Sensitive relay controlled by 1 output bit from the
Sinclair. The number with an asterisk refers to the Radio
Shack part number at the time of this writing. Contacts
are rated at one ampere each for 110 VAC.

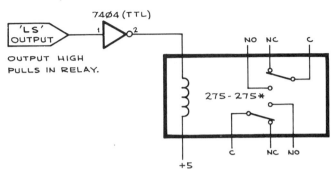

More recently mechanical relays have been eclipsed by solid-state relays. These relays consist of a light-emitting diode placed next to a light-sensitive triac. Since the only connection between the diode and the triac is a light path, solid-state relays provide excellent isolation. They are much faster than mechanical relays and are much more reliable, since there are no moving parts. The top panel of Figure 4-13 on p. 52 shows a MOC 3010 optocoupled triac used to switch AC devices. We can use it to control a power triac, as shown in the figure. That simple circuit can control up to 600 watts and costs under $3. The bottom figure shows the same circuit adapted for an inductive load, such as a motor. High-powered solid-state relays that can control up to 10 amps are available and cost between $10 and $20. They are sold at most industrial electronics supply houses.

FIGURE 4-13

Triac output. 1 output bit can control up to a 6-ampere-110VAC load. The numbers with asterisks refer to Radio Shack part numbers at the time of this printing. The top circuit is for resistive loads while the bottom one is for inductive loads, such as transformers and motors.

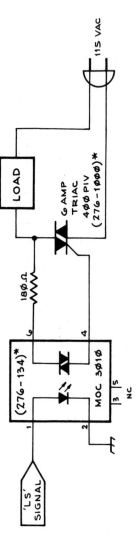

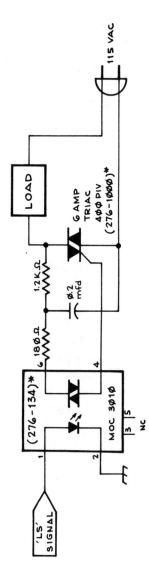

5

PARALLEL INPUT PORTS

In Chapter 4 we discussed a general-purpose parallel output port. This chapter will describe the parallel input port. As its name implies, the parallel input port takes 8 bits of data into the computer simultaneously. Since many computer peripheral devices—such as paper-tape readers, card readers, digital-to-analog converters, and so on—generate a multiple-bit binary signal, such a port is very useful. In addition, like the parallel output port, the parallel input port can be utilized as 8 independent inputs, with each input assigned a different function, depending on what the inputs have been connected to.

Principles of data capture

In the chapter on output ports (chapter 4) we found that the Z80 put the binary pattern of the word to be output on the 8 data lines for a brief period of time. Signals on the address lines alerted the device that data was coming to it, and the actual timing of the data transfer was accomplished by a data-transfer strobe. The strobe caused the device to latch the data off the data lines at the precise time when the Z80 asserted it. Data transfer into the Z80 is the exact reverse of that procedure. In this case the external device will be alerted by the proper address on the address bus that the Z80 wants to read data from it. An input data-transfer strobe tells the device to deposit its data on the data lines while the strobe is in the active state. Latches in the Z80 then capture it. The input data-transfer strobe is, in turn, generated by the condition where the READ line and the MREQ are both low.

3-State devices

The next question is how can the input device assert its output only during the strobe pulse? To answer this we must examine the nature of the Z80's data bus more closely.

The data bus is what we call a *bidirectional bus*; that is, data flows both into and out of the Z80 over the same 8 wires. The direction of flow at any given time is indicated by the READ and WRITE lines. If neither are low, then no data transfers are occurring. Thus each data line is at one time an output line and at other times an input line. This multiple usage is accomplished by utilizing 3-state technology. A 3-state device is, as its name implies, a device with 3 logic states. These states are a logic low, a logic high, and a special high-impedance state. In the high-impedance state, it is as if the line were disconnected from the output of the logic circuit. Many 3-state outputs may be tied together as long as no more than 1 leaves the high-impedance state at any given time. When data is being output over the data lines, they are in a low-impedance mode and are asserting the lines to their proper logic levels. External devices are made aware of this by a logic low on the WRITE line from the Z80. When an external device is to send data into the Z80, the data-transfer strobe must cause the selected device's 3-state outputs to leave the high-impedance mode and assert the data lines. Thus all input devices must communicate with the data bus through 3-state logic.

Figure 4-8 (p. 48) shows the pin assignments and the truth tables for the 74LS125 and the 74LS126 3-state buffers. Each package contains 4 independently controlled 3-state noninverting buffers. The only difference between the 2 is the polarity of the control gate. The 74LS125 is in the high-impedance state when the control gate is high, while the 74LS126 is in the high-impedance state when the control gate is low.

Constructing a parallel input port

Figure 5-2 shows a schematic for a simple general-purpose parallel input port. A strobe pulse is generated whenever both the device address is true (Pin 9 of the 74LS138 ROM decoder described in Chapter 3) and the READ line is low. 74LS126s were used since a positive strobe pulse is generated,

FIGURE 5-1

Input timing for the Z80. The point when the chip is selected and $\overline{MREQ}$ goes low to the point when the peripheral asserts valid data on the data bus is the access time. One T cycle in the Sinclair is about 800ns.

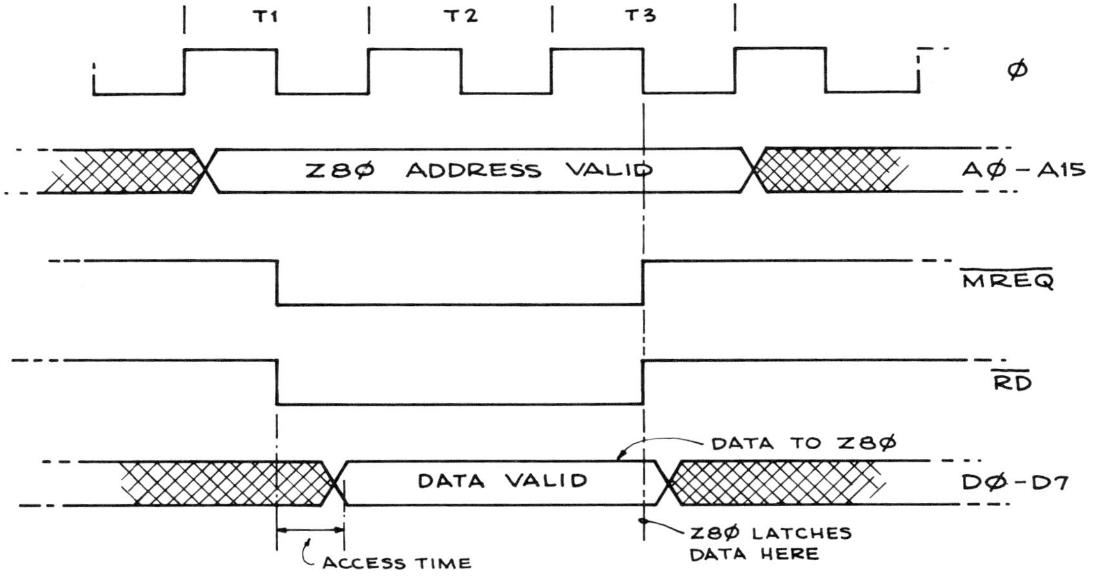

ϕ

$A\phi - A15$

$\overline{MREQ}$

$\overline{RD}$

$D\phi - D7$

T1   T2   T3

Z8ϕ ADDRESS VALID

DATA VALID

DATA TO Z8ϕ

Z8ϕ LATCHES
DATA HERE

ACCESS TIME

FIGURE 5-2

Parallel input port schematic. The resistors and switches are only required for the experiments. See Figure 3-3 for the ROM decoder.

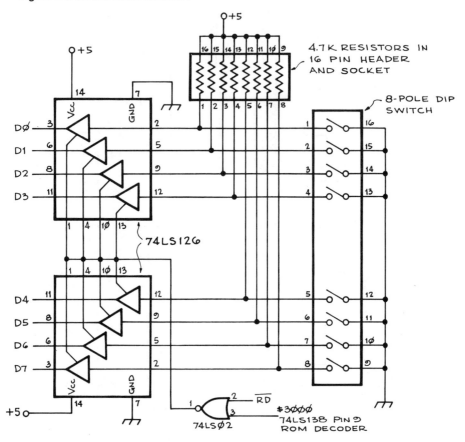

but 74LS125 could also be used by simply inverting the strobe pulse. We also show 8 pull-up resistors and switches in the diagram. These resistors and switches are not actually a part of the input port but rather serve only as a means of putting a known bit pattern on the input port. If you plan to perform the following input-port exercises, then we suggest you include the resistors and switches as shown.

Wire the sockets as shown in Figure 5-2 and insert the integrated circuits. Be sure that all power and ground pins from the ICs have been properly connected. The reader should be reminded at this point that some errors in wiring could cause damage to your computer. When you are satisfied that your wiring is correct, plug the expansion board into the computer.

56

Plug the expansion board into your Sinclair computer and turn it on. Check immediately to see if the cursor appears on the screen. If it does not, turn off the power. You have a wiring error. Double check your work and correct the problem. Proceed with the initial checkout by opening all 8 switches and executing the following command:

PRINT PEEK 12288

A 255 should appear on the screen. Now close all 8 switches and repeat the command. If a 0 appears, the port is working correctly.

Exercises with the input port

The POKE command caused the binary representation of the decimal data to appear on the 8 output lines. Similarly the PEEK command returns a decimal representation of the binary data that was present on the 8 input lines. This procedure can be illustrated with the following program:

```
10 SCROLL
20 PRINT PEEK 12288
30 GOTO 10
```

Enter the program, close all 8 switches, and start the program. The screen should fill with 0s. Now open switch 1. Note that the 0s are replaced with 1s. Switch 1 is on the data line DO, the 1 weight bit. Now close switch 1 and open switch 2. Note that 2s now appear on the screen. This is because switch 2 is the 2 weight bit. The following table shows the bit weight for each of the 8 switches. Verify that the table is correct by opening each switch and observing the computer's output.

Switch number	1	2	3	4	5	6	7	8
Bit weight	1	2	4	8	16	32	64	128

Combinations of switch openings will produce the sum of the bit weights. For example, opening switches 1 and 3 will yield the sum of 1 and 4, which is 5 to be read by the computer. Try it. What is returned when switches 4 and 5 are open? Try various combinations such that you can cause any number you wish to appear on the screen.

A handy use for the parallel input port is to monitor 8 individual events. In this case, you are more concerned with whether an individual switch is open or closed than with the decimal number returned by the

PEEK statement. The following program determines the status of the 8 input lines. Enter the program and start it. Note that the 8 bits on the screen are exactly the same as the ones on the switches.

```
10 DIM F (8)
20 LET N = PEEK 12288
30 SCROLL
40 LET T = 128
50 FOR J = 1 TO 8
60 IF N >= T THEN GOTO 90
70 LET F (J) = 0
80 GOTO 110
90 LET N = N - T
100 LET F (J) = 1
110 LET T = T/2
120 PRINT F (J);
130 NEXT J
140 GOTO 20
```

The program works by testing if the number under consideration is equal to or larger than 128. If it is, then bit 7 was a 1. If not, then bit 7 was a 0. If bit 7 was set, then 128 is subtracted from N and the remainder is compared to 64 to see if bit 6 is set. This process continues until all 8 bits are checked. Lines 40 through 130 could easily be used as a subroutine to check the 8 bits. The display can be suppressed by removing line 120, in which case the bits are represented by the 8-member array of Fs. For example, if F (4) is a 1, then bit 4 was set. If F (4) is a 0, then bit 4 was not set.

Unwired bits

In this example we put 3-state buffers on all 8 data lines to bring in an 8-bit word. However, if your application requires less than 8 bits of information, then only the number of data bits required need be wired. All unwired data lines will assume a logic 1 state in the Sinclair computer. To prove this, close all 8 switches and execute:

PRINT PEEK 12288

You should see a 0 printed on the screen. Now turn off the power and remove the 3-state buffer on data lines 0 to 3. Turn the computer back on and repeat

PRINT PEEK 12288

Note that a 15 is now printed. Data lines 0 through 3 were not asserted but were allowed to float at the time of the read; thus the computer read 1 + 2 + 4 + 8, or 15. A single-bit input port tied to data line 7 will yield a 127 on the 0 condition and a 255 on the 1 condition.

Multiple input ports

In Chapter 4 we found that additional output ports could be added to the Sinclair computer by simply decoding the address bus deeper and deeper. The same is true of the input ports. As long as the data-transfer strobes are unique for each device, an almost unlimited number of input ports can be interfaced. Furthermore since 3-state buffers in the high-impedance mode offer a minimal load to the data lines, the loading problem we encountered with multiple-output ports is not a major factor.

Figures 5-3 and 5-4 show 2 address-decoding schemes, one generating 2 input ports and the other 8 ports. Note that these schemes are identical to those presented for the output port except that READ is used in place of WRITE. The outputs of these circuits can be tied directly to the controls of 74LS125s or 74LS126s.

Bidirectional ports

Although you cannot have 2 separate input devices decoded for the same address, it is all right for an input and an output device to share the same

FIGURE 5-3
Decoding for 2 ports. The upper strobe will respond to addresses between $3000 and $33FF while the lower one will respond to those between $3400 and $37FF. Note how inverters can be used if a negative strobe pulse is required. See Figure 3-3 for the ROM decoder.

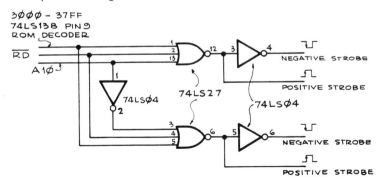

FIGURE 5-4

8-port decoder schematic. This circuit enables 8 read strobes at the hex addresses shown. A 74LS04 is shown on line $3000–$30FF to illustrate how a positive strobe can be generated, if needed, on any of the 8 lines.

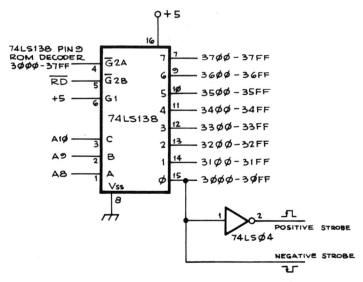

address. In fact, this sharing is a common practice in computer design. For example, CRT terminals are traditionally interfaced so that the screen is the output side and the keyboard is the input side of the same address. The epitome of this practice is in memory, where every word occupies the same input and output address.

Sensing non-TTL level inputs

If you are interfacing to a device that supplies TTL level signals, then all that is required is to tie those signals to the inputs of the 3-state buffers. Many devices we wish to interface, however, do not have TTL logic levels. We have already shown you how to sense a switch closure in Figure 5-2. In this case, the standard procedure is to use a pull-up resistor on the line and a switch closure to ground. An open switch causes a logic 1 and closure a logic 0. If you wish to sense a signal that is either outside the 0–5 volt range of the logic chips or is of such a high impedance that it will not drive a 3-state buffer, a voltage comparator IC will usually solve the problem. Figure 5-5 shows an LM311 comparator in use as an input conditioner. If the voltage on the noninverting input is greater than that on the inverting input, then the output is a logic 0, or 0 volts. If the inverting input has the

FIGURE 5-5

A comparator as an input conditioner. Note that the output will be high when the input is above the threshold and low when it is below the threshold. An unregulated supply like the one shown in Figure 11-3 can be used for the ± 15 volts.

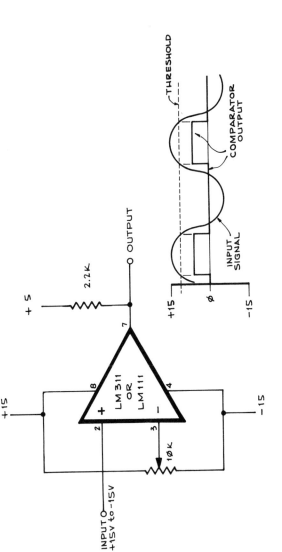

greatest voltage, then the output is a logic 1 (5 volts). The comparator is very sensitive and only a few millivolts' difference between the inputs can be detected. Note that the LM311 is an open collector device. Therefore, it requires a 2.2K pull-up resistor between its output and +5 volts. The potentiometer must be set such that a threshold voltage is selected that is approximately halfway between the 2 voltage states expected. This circuit will work with input voltages in the range of +15 to −15 volts and will draw only a few microamperes from the voltage source. If your signal exceeds the ± 15-volt range, then you must attenuate it with a resistor network first to bring it into that range.

Handshaking

Data transfer between a computer and an external device often requires very critical timing. For example, if you had interfaced your computer to a card reader, the computer would need to know when a card had been read and that data was available. Furthermore the card reader would need to know when the computer had taken the data so that it could proceed to the next card. This communication between device and computer is called *handshaking*. Handshaking is usually accomplished with two signals— data available and data received. The data-available line comes from the external device and changes state when the data is stable on its output. Let's assume that the data-available line was wired to bit 7 of an input port at 12289 and that the 8-bit data word came into an input port wired at 12288. Furthermore let's assume that a high on the data-available line means data is ready to be taken by the computer. Finally a high on the data-received line means that the computer has taken the data and that it may proceed to the next task. Figure 5-6 shows an interface that can handle the handshaking when used with the following program code:

```
100 IF PEEK 12289 < 128 GOTO 100
110 LET X = PEEK 12288
```

In line 100 the program loops until data line 7 goes high with the data-available signal. Once this happens, a 255 will be read and the program will proceed to line 110 where the data is actually read. The data-available signal also sets the data-received line low. When the data is read into the computer, the strobe toggles the flip-flop so that the data-received line is set back to a high, thus completing the handshake.

FIGURE 5-6

Handshaking schematic. Timing between the peripheral and the computer is accomplished by the peripheral telling the computer when it has data available and the computer telling the device when it has taken the data. Reading the data also clears the flip-flop, indicating data received. Data available resets the flip-flop.

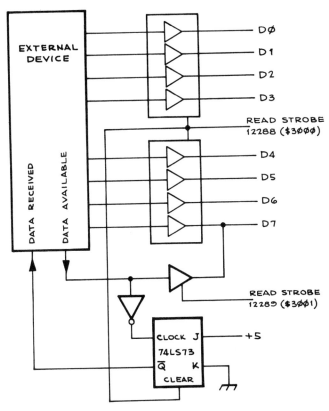

FIGURE 5-7

Data for the 74LS73. Courtesy Motorola Semiconductor Products, Inc.

74LS73A

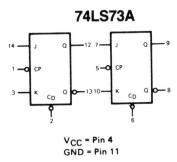

V_{CC} = Pin **4**
GND = Pin 11

6

HANDLING
ANALOG SIGNALS

Many of us grew up very mystified by computers. They were something incredibly complex that lurked in the basements of the big universities. Because of the expense involved with the computers of just 10 years ago, only an elite few actually had access to them and were allowed to discover that they are easily understood and can make good pets. The rest of us could only gaze with wonderment at this mystery called a computer, which was filled with secrecy and wrapped in an enigma. Whenever someone would try to explain computers in those days, it would start out, "Well, Johnny, there are 2 types of computers: digital and analog." Today the general-purpose analog computers have gone the way of the dinosaurs, but unfortunately not before the word *analog* became just as foreboding as *digital* or as *computer* itself.

What is an analog signal?

Actually the term analog has a simple meaning that really has nothing to do with computers per se. An analog signal is simply one whose value is continuously variable. For example, the voltage in the wall socket is continuously changing between about +155 and −155 volts. Unlike a digital signal, which has only 2 defined states—+5 or 0 volts, the voltage may be anywhere between the 2 extremes mentioned, depending on the time at which the voltage is sampled. Most of us are much more familiar with analog signals than with digital signals. The gas gauge on your car, a conventional wall clock, a mercury thermometer—these are all analog devices; some are electric, and others are purely mechanical. Because we really live in an analog world, the problem "How can I get my digital computer to monitor or to produce an analog signal?" becomes a common one. The most straightforward solution to this problem is to interface a digital-to-analog or an analog-to-digital converter to the Sinclair. These interfaces are described here.

Digital-to-analog conversion

Some of the devices we would like the Sinclair to control require an analog rather than a digital signal. Such applications might include driving an X-Y plotter, varying the voltage on the lamp in a photo enlarger, or perhaps producing a signal for a motor speed control. Such applications will require a digital-to-analog converter (DAC). As the name implies, a DAC produces an analog voltage that is proportional to the binary signal on its input. A popular and inexpensive DAC is the Motorola MC1408. It is interchangeable with the Analog Device AD559 or the National Semiconductor DAC0808. It is an 8-bit DAC, so it can vary its output over a range of 256 discrete steps. This means that it can produce a voltage that will be within half a percent of the required value.

Figure 6-1 shows how a simple 4-bit DAC works. A series of precision resistors are arranged in parallel and can be switched in or out of the circuit by MOS switches. These resistors are called the *ladder network*. Each element has twice the resistance of the resistor above it. The MOS switch on the lowest resistor is controlled by the most significant bit of the binary signal, while the highest resistance in the ladder is controlled by the least significant byte. The input current of the op-amp will be in proportion to the binary pattern on the switches, since each switch controls a resistance that is reciprocally related to the weight of that bit. The output voltage of the op-amp will, in turn, be equal to the input current times the feedback resistance, R_F.

The MC1408 contains an 8-bit ladder network and the control switches. You must provide the op-amp and a set of digital latches to get the signal off the data bus. Figure 6-2 shows a 2-channel DAC interfaced to the Sinclair. The binary data is latched off the data bus by 74LS75 D flip-flops. A 74LS138 decodes the low-order address lines A0–A2 to produce strobes for 8 consecutive addresses. The first address, 12288, controls the top

FIGURE 6-1
A theoretical 4-bit DAC.

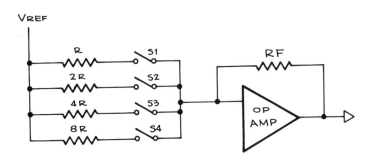

DAC; the second, 12289, controls the second DAC; and the third strobes a 4-bit latch to provide 4 control signals, such as a pen lift. The latched data controls the 2 DACs. A 3-volt Zener diode provides a precision reference voltage for the ladder networks. Finally the outputs of the ladder networks go to 741 op-amps.

Initial checkout of DAC

Wire the IC sockets as shown in Figure 6-2 and install all the discrete components, such as resistors and capacitors. Note that a ±12 to ±15 volt supply is required for the op-amp. This supply need not be highly regulated; the simple circuit shown in Figure 11-3 would be suitable. When the circuit is completed, put the 74LS138 in its socket and leave all the other sockets empty. Turn on the Sinclair and the ± 12 volt supply. Check to see that a cursor appears on the monitor. Once this is verified, check to see that 3 volts are present at Pin 14 of the 2 1408 sockets. If not, check the Zener diode to see if it is improperly wired or in backward. Next insert the 741 and check the output of the op-amps. They should have 0 volts on their outputs. If not, double check their wiring. Next turn off the power and insert all the rest of the ICs. Turn on the power and verify that a cursor appears on the screen. Enter and run the following program:

```
 5 SLOW
10 FOR J = 1 to 255
20 POKE 12288, J
30 POKE 12289, J
40 NEXT J
50 GOTO 10
```

67

FIGURE 6-2
Schematic for a 2-channel DAC. Note that 4 digital flags are also included that can be used for pen-lift signals and so on. The Analog Devices AD559, or National Semiconductor DAC 0808 are pin-compatible substitutes for the MC1408.

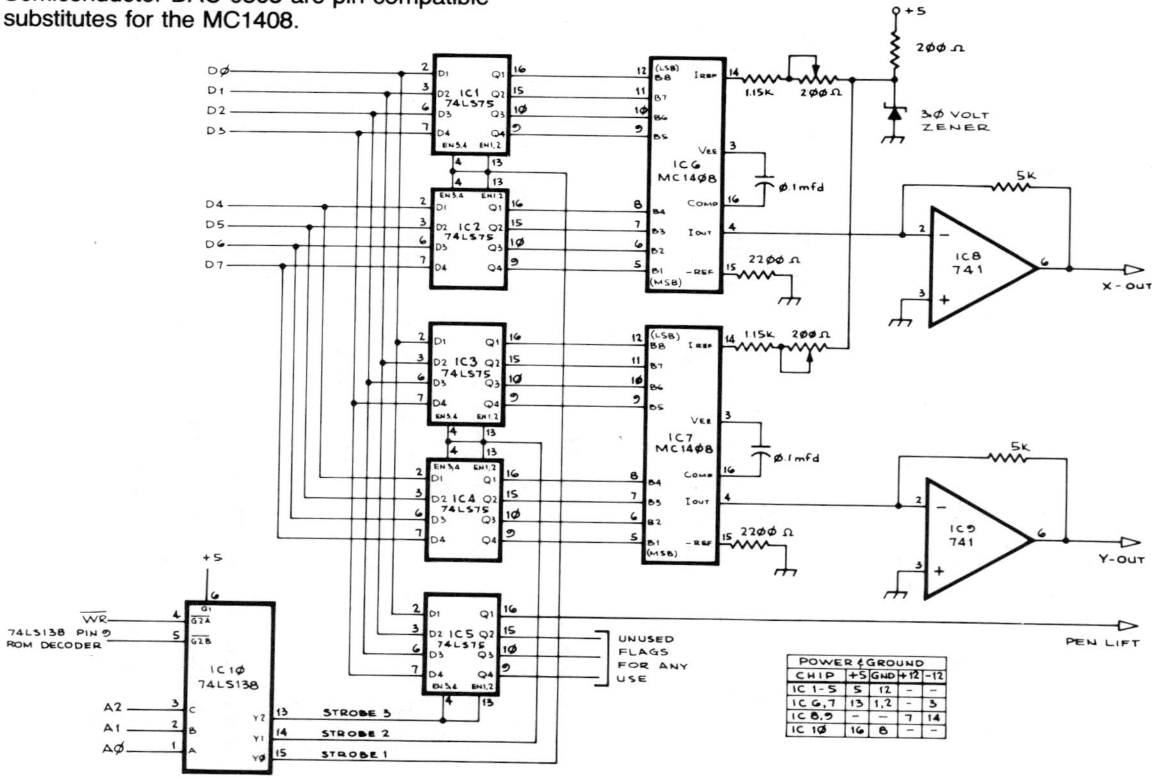

POWER & GROUND				
CHIP	+5	GND	+12	-12
IC 1-5	5	12	–	–
IC 6,7	13	1,2	–	3
IC 8,9	–	–	7	14
IC 10	16	8	–	–

Put a probe on the output of each op-amp. A slow ramp should be seen going from 0 volts to -10 volts and then quickly resetting to 0. If this signal is lacking from either channel, check for strobe pulses on Pins 4 and 13 of the 74LS75s with a logic probe. If these pulses are present, check for latched data on Pins 9, 10, 15, and 16 of the 74LS75s with the logic probe. If all these tests check out, double check the wiring of the MC1408 sockets.

Output characteristics of the DAC

The full range of these DACs is from 0 volts, when a 0 is POKEd, to $+10$ volts, when a 255 is POKEd. This range can be altered by changing the feedback resistor on the 741 op-amp. For example, if 2.5K is used, the full range would be 0 to $+5$ volts. If 500 ohms were used, then the full range would be 0 to $+1$ volts. If you want the output to be bipolar, simply put a 20K pot between the inverting input of the 741 (Pin 2) and -12 volts. POKE a 128 to that DAC and adjust the pot for 0 volts output. Now, with a 5K feedback resistor, 255 will produce -5 volts and 0 will produce $+5$ volts.

Graphic plotting using the DAC

A very useful application for the DAC is to create graphic output using an analog X–Y plotter. X–Y plotting is accomplished by connecting the output of one of the DACs to the X channel and the output of the other to the Y channel of the plotter. Finally attach the programmable flag to the pen lift.

The heart of any plotting package is a subroutine that draws a vector between any 2 points. The following program has such a routine starting at line 1000. In this example, the X-DAC is at address 12288 and the Y-DAC is at 12289. The pen is lifted when a 0 is POKEd to 12290 and is dropped to the paper with a 1.

The subroutine draws a straight line from the pen's previous position to the new coordinates of X and Y. If Z = 0, the pen is lifted before the move, and if it is a 1, the pen stays down so that a straight line is drawn from the old XY coordinate to the new one. The line is drawn by calculating closely spaced points along the line and outputting these to the DACs in rapid succession. The main program lines 5–170 draw the set of axes and the parabola shown in Figure 6-3.

FIGURE 6-3
Parabola plot. The top panel shows the plot when the
pen lift is disconnected. The bottom panel shows the
completed plot.

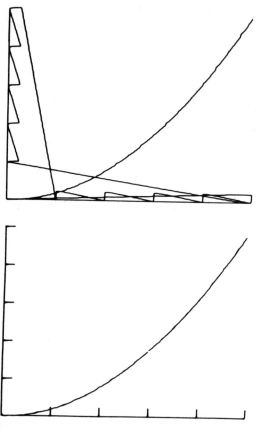

LISTING 6-1

```
 5 REM DRAW AXIS
10 LET Z=0
11 LET X=0
12 LET Y=200
13 REM GOSUB 1090 FOR FIRST CALL TO SET UP
   VARIABLES
14 GOSUB 1090
15 GOSUB 1000
20 LET Z=1
21 LET Y=0
```

```
23 GOSUB 1000
30 LET X=200
31 GOSUB 1000
35 REM DRAW HASH MARKS
40 FOR I=1 TO 5
50 LET Z=0
51 LET X=0
52 LET Y=40*I
53 GOSUB 1000
60 LET Z=1
61 LET X=10
62 GOSUB 1000
70 NEXT I
80 FOR I=1 TO 5
90 LET Z=0
91 LET Y=0
92 LET X=I*40
93 GOSUB 1000
100 LET Z=1
101 LET Y=10
102 GOSUB 1000
110 NEXT I
120 REM DRAW CURVE
130 LET X=0
131 LET Y=0
132 GOSUB 1000
135 LET Z=1
140 FOR I=1 TO 20
150 LET X=I*10
151 LET Y=(I**2)/2
152 GOSUB 1000
160 NEXT I
161 LET Z=0
162 GOSUB 1000
170 STOP

998 REM VECTOR ROUTINE
999 REM V3 IS X OLD, V5 IS Y OLD
1000 POKE 12290,Z
1004 LET V6=Y-V5
1005 LET V4=X-V3
```

```
1006 REM V1 IS HYPOTENUSE
1010 LET V1=SQR ((V4*V4)+(V6*V6))
1015 REM CHECK FOR ZERO MOVE
1020 IF V1<1 THEN GOTO 1090
1040 LET V7=V4/V1
1045 LET V8=V6/V1
1050 FOR V=1 TO V1
1070 LET V3=V3+V7
1071 LET V5=V5+V8
1080 POKE 12288,V3
1081 POKE 12289,V5
1082 NEXT V
1090 LET V3=X
1091 LET V5=Y
1100 RETURN
```

In the preceding program we broke the curve into 20 short line segments. More complex functions can be plotted by calculating the X and Y values in closely spaced intervals. When smaller calculations are made, the pen appears to move in a continuous sweep rather than in small jerky steps. The following program illustrates this principle by plotting a rose. This innovative program was adapted from Michael Zron's article entitled "Superrose" in the April, 1979 issue of *Creative Computing* (pp. 98–99). Supply integer values for A and B between 1 and 10. Figure 6-4 shows some plots generated by the program.

LISTING 6-2

```
  1 REM ROSE PLOTTER
  5 CLS
 10 LET X = 0
 20 LET Y = 0
 30 GOSUB 1000
 40 PRINT "ENTER 2 INTEGERS A AND B"
 50 PRINT "THEY MUST BE BETWEEN 1 AND 10"
 60 PRINT
 70 PRINT
 80 PRINT "ENTER A"
 90 INPUT A
100 CLS
```

FIGURE 6-4
Several plots from the rose program

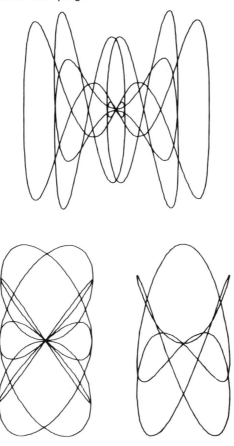

```
 110 PRINT "ENTER B"
 120 INPUT B
 130 FOR I = 0 TO 2* 3.1415 STEP 3.1415/180
 140 LET R = 12* SIN (T * 3)
 150 LET X =10 * R * COS (A * T)
 160 LET Y =10 * R * SIN (B * T)
 170 GOSUB 1000
 180 NEXT T
 190 STOP
1000 POKE 12288, X + 128
1010 POKE 12289, Y + 128
1020 RETURN
```

73

Analog-to-digital conversion

As its name implies, the analog-to-digital converter (ADC) generates a multiple-bit binary signal that is proportional to the voltage it is monitoring. The heart of the ADC is the digital-to-analog converter (DAC) previously described. Instead of having the computer control the DAC, however, the ADC has its own internal computer circuit called the *successive approximation logic*. When the ADC is started, the successive approximation logic sends a bit pattern to the DAC. The voltage generated by the DAC is then compared to the input voltage. The result of this comparison is then sent to the successive approximation logic so that a new bit pattern can be generated that will bring the DAC's voltage closer to the input. When the DAC's voltage is as close as it can be to the input, the successive approximation logic sends an end-of-conversion signal to the computer. The computer responds by reading the bit pattern on the DAC through a parallel port.

A valuable addition to an ADC is a multiple-channel multiplexer, or MUX. The MUX selects 1 of many input signals to be converted. As shown in Figure 6-5, it can be thought of as a multiple pole switch that can be set by the computer. Because the computer can sample a voltage very quickly through the ADC, the addition of a MUX will allow the computer to rotate through the sampling of several analog signals and give the appearance of simultaneously measuring all the signals.

The ADC0816 chip

Until recently, ADCs were expensive and out of the reach of most experimenters. Furthermore they were quite complex and difficult to interface. These problems have happily been overcome, however, with the advent of National Semiconductor's ADC0816 chip, which puts an entire analog-to-digital converter on a single chip. 3-state outputs and a 16-channel input multiplexer have also been thrown into this chip just for good measure. At the time of this writing, these chips are available for about $20 each. Although many other analog-to-digital converters are on the market, we feel that the ADC0816 is by far the most cost effective of them all.

The ADC0816 is an 8-bit converter; that is, it will discriminate to 1 part in 2^8 (256). This precision is better than one-half percent accuracy (which is usually good enough for most applications). It also conveniently mates with the 8-bit word structure of the Z80's data bus. The ADC0816 will complete a conversion in under 100 microseconds. Figure 6-7 shows the ADC0816 interfaced to a Sinclair computer. Note that the write strobe

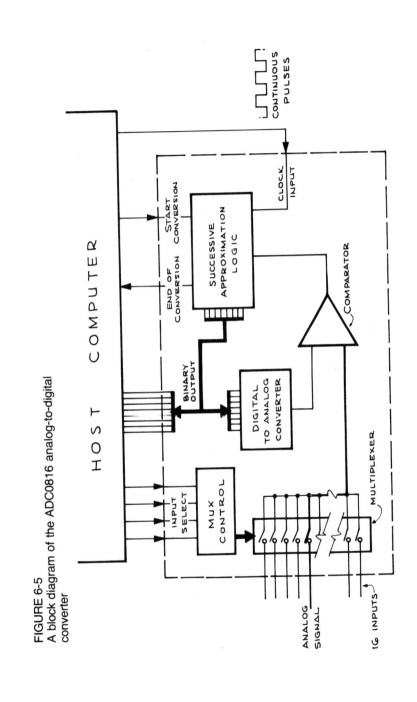

FIGURE 6-5
A block diagram of the ADC0816 analog-to-digital converter

FIGURE 6-6
Data for ADC0816

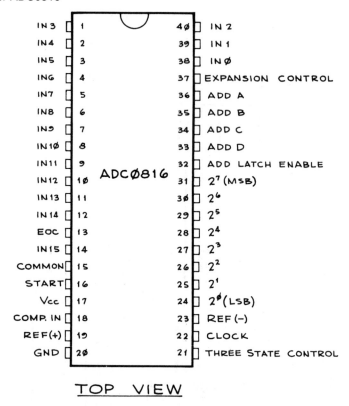

IN 3	1	40	IN 2
IN 4	2	39	IN 1
IN 5	3	38	IN 0
IN 6	4	37	EXPANSION CONTROL
IN 7	5	36	ADD A
IN 8	6	35	ADD B
IN 9	7	34	ADD C
IN 10	8	33	ADD D
IN 11	9	32	ADD LATCH ENABLE
IN 12	10	31	2^7 (MSB)
IN 13	11	30	2^6
IN 14	12	29	2^5
EOC	13	28	2^4
IN 15	14	27	2^3
COMMON	15	26	2^2
START	16	25	2^1
Vcc	17	24	2^0 (LSB)
COMP. IN	18	23	REF (−)
REF (+)	19	22	CLOCK
GND	20	21	THREE STATE CONTROL

ADC0816

TOP VIEW

goes to both the address latch enable (ALE) of the multiplexer and the start pin. The multiplexer address select is latched from the 4 low-order address lines on the rising edge of the strobe pulse and the successive approximation logic is started on the falling edge. In this scheme a POKE to 12288–12304 ($3000–$300F) will select 1 of the 16 channels in the multiplexer and start the converter. A PEEK to 12288 will retrieve the answer once the conversion is completed. An end-of-conversion signal (EOC) is available from the ADC0816 but is not interfaced to the computer for the simple reason that the Sinclair takes much longer than the 100 microseconds conversion time to execute a PEEK statement after a POKE statement. Thus, using BASIC, it would be impossible to try to read the ADC before the conversion has been completed. If, however, you plan to program the ADC in machine language, then it will be necessary to interface the EOC signal and have the machine-language program check its status before reading the ADC's output. This modification is shown in

FIGURE 6-7
Schematic for the ADC. Don't forget power and grounds
on the 74LS02. Refer to Figure 6-6 for multiplexer input
pins.

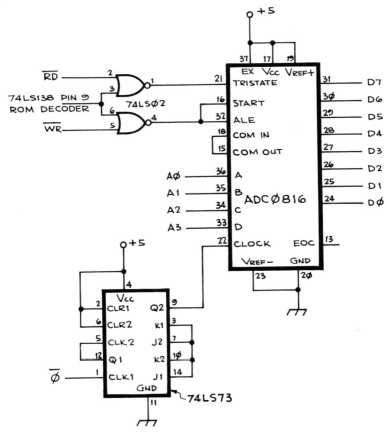

Figure 6-8. In this scheme, the EOC signal is detected by reading address
$3001. A not-ready condition will be indicated by a 0 on bit 7. A data-ready
condition will be indicated by bit 7 being a 1.

In Figure 6-8, we have tied REF (+) and REF (−) to Vcc and ground,
respectively. The precision of the analog-to-digital converter will depend
on the precision and stability of these voltages in your system. For example, if there is 60 hertz ripple on your board's +5 volts, then the reproduci-
bility of the ADC will be affected, since REF (+) and REF (−) are the
internal reference voltages for the converter's DAC. If you find that you
cannot obtain the degree of accuracy you desire in your system, you then
should consider adding a precision voltage source like the one shown in
Figure 6-9. Note that the reference supply is set for 5.12 volts rather than an

FIGURE 6-8

End-of-conversion modification. Bit 7 of address $3001 will contain the end-of-conversion flag. When bit 7 becomes set, the data is ready to be taken. Converted data is at $3000.

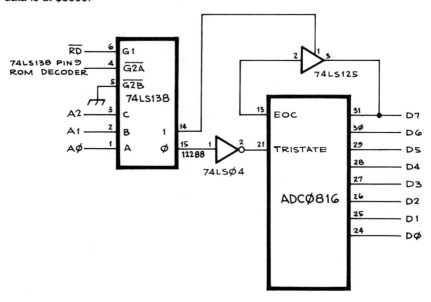

FIGURE 6-9

A reference voltage source for the ADC0816

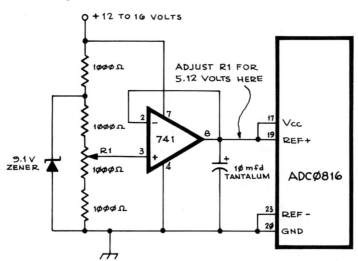

even 5 volts. This setting has the simple advantage that 256, the maximum capacity of the 8-bit word, is an even multiple of 5.12. Thus each bit of the converted value will equal 5.12/256 or 0.02 volts. If you use the 5-volt supply as the reference, the calibration factor will be 5.00/256 or .01953, which is slightly less convenient. We have found that the regulated 5 volts on our expansion board was quite suitable for all but the most demanding of applications. Finally the ADC0816 needs a .5 to 1 mHz clock. This clock was generated by dividing the system clock Φ by 4 with a 74LS73 dual JK flip-flop.

Checkout of the ADC

Make the connections as shown in Figure 6-7. Double check the connections to put the 74LS02 and the 74LS73 in their sockets. Be sure all power and ground pins to the ICs are properly connected. Again the reader should be warned that errors in wiring could damage your computer. Plug the expansion board into the computer. Turn on the monitor and turn on the Sinclair. Check to see that the cursor appears on the monitor. If it does not, turn off the power and locate the wiring error before proceeding. Now turn off the power and put the ADC0816 in its socket. You will need a test voltage that can be varied between 0 and +5 volts. The wiper of a 10K pot between system power and ground does nicely. Put the voltage source on Pin 38 (input 0) of the ADC0816. Turn off the computer and again verify that a cursor is present. Enter the following program and start it.

```
10 POKE 12288, 0
20 SCROLL
30 PRINT PEEK 12288
40 GO TO 10
```

Numbers should be scrolling up the screen. As you change the input voltage, the numbers should change in proportion to the input voltage. If no response is obtained, you should proceed as follows:

1. Is there a start pulse? Check Pin 16 on the ADC with a logic probe while the preceding program is running. The line should be low with very short positive pulses. The pulses should stop when the program is stopped.
2. Is there a read strobe? Check Pin 21 on the ADC with the logic probe

as the program runs. The line should have short pulses like the start pin. If not, check the read-strobe circuit and locate the problem.

3. Is the multiplexer working? Check Pin 38 on the ADC with a voltmeter and see if it varies as the test voltage is varied. After this condition is verified, place the voltmeter on Pin 15, the output of the multiplexer. This voltage should be the same as the input voltage on Pin 38. If not, check the address lines, Pins 33 to 36, to see if they are wired correctly.

4. Is the converter working? With the logic probe, check for clock pulses on Pin 22 of the ADC. If these are present, start the preceding program and check for an EOC pulse on Pin 13. Lack of a pulse here indicates that the converter is not working. If all these tests were met but no EOC pulse is present, then your ADC0816 chip may be defective.

Programming the ADC

The ADC0816 is very easy to program in BASIC and will require machine-language programming in only the most unusual circumstances. The converter is started by a POKE to an address between 12288 and 12303. The channel selected depends on the address POKEd. For example, a POKE to 12288 will select channel 0. This channel is selected because address lines 0–3, which are connected to the multiplexer inputs, will all have 0s. A POKE to 12289 will select channel 1, a POKE to 12290 will select channel 2, and so forth. The following code shows how this series of POKEs could be programmed:

```
10 PRINT "CHANNEL #";
20 INPUT N
30 POKE (12288 + N), 0
```

The second argument of the POKE serves no function as nothing is read from the data lines at that time by the ADC0816. Therefore a 0 has been placed there in the preceding program. The converted value can then be read by a PEEK statement following the POKE. The conversion takes less than 200 microseconds, and there is no need to worry about trying to read the data before it is ready since BASIC is not that fast in Sinclair computers.

Many analog-to-digital conversion applications require sampling at preset time intervals. The internal 60 hertz clock of the ZX81 and Timex models can be used to accomplish this timing. The following code causes the ADC to take 100 samples at a rate of two per second.

```
10 DIM X (100)
20 FAST
100 FOR J = 1 TO 100
110 POKE 11288, 0
120 LET X(J) = PEEK 12288
130 PAUSE 29
140 NEXT J
```

Note that a delay of 29/60ths of a second occurs in line 130. The remaining 1/60th of a second is occupied in program overhead. In the FAST mode we found that it takes .014 seconds to execute the lines 110 and 130 in a FOR-NEXT loop, which is pretty close to the .0166 second required for 1 jiffy.

Analog input conditioning

The ADC0816 has a high impedance input and accepts a signal between 0 and +5 volts. If your signal falls in that range, then nothing further will be needed. More often than not, however, the signal you wish to measure will fall outside that range. For this reason, some input conditioning will probably be required. If the signal is greater than +5 volts in amplitude and does not swing negative, then a simple resistive attenuator, as shown in Figure 6-10, will do. The design rules are: select a desired input impedance, solve for R_2 with equation 1, and then solve for R_1 with equation 2.

If your signal swings negative or is considerably less than 5 volts, then an op-amp circuit will be needed, as shown in Figure 6-11. This circuit provides an offset shift to accommodate negative as well as positive signals and scales the signal such that the full input range produces a swing between 0 and 5 volts for the ADC0816. The pot is an offset adjustment; it should be adjusted so that 0 volts (input grounded) yields a converted value of 128, half scale. Note that the op-amp inverts the signal as well as scaling it so that negative voltages of the input will yield converted values between 128 and 255. Positive voltages will yield values between 0 and 128. The polarity can be restored in software along with the scale factor. For example, suppose that a reference of 5.00 volts is used for the ADC and RIN is 40K. By equation 1 in Figure 6-11, this value will accommodate an input signal between $+1$ and -1 volts. The following code samples a voltage on channel 1 and sets X equal to its value in volts.

```
100 POKE 12288,0
110 LET X = (128 − PEEK 12288) * (1/128)
```

FIGURE 6-10
Input attenuator for ADC. Solve for R_1 and R_2 in the circuit by providing the desired input impedance, Z, (be realistic) and the maximum signal voltage, E in (max).

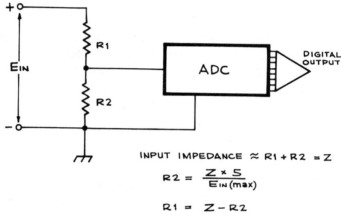

$$\text{INPUT IMPEDANCE} \approx R1 + R2 = Z$$

$$R2 = \frac{Z \times 5}{E_{IN}(max)}$$

$$R1 = Z - R2$$

FIGURE 6-11
Op-amp signal conditioner. Use this circuit when E in (max) is either less than 5 volts or when the signal is bipolar.

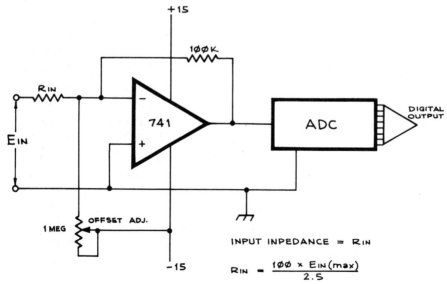

$$\text{INPUT INPEDANCE} = R_{IN}$$

$$R_{IN} = \frac{100 \times E_{IN}(max)}{2.5}$$

7

JOYSTICKS

A very popular interfacing project is adding joysticks to your computer. Joysticks are very useful for the implementation of action games, such as Space Invaders, that require user-coordinated responses difficult to effect through the keyboard. Furthermore the principles of the interfaces we will present for joysticks can be used to detect any type of switch closure or resistance change. These applications could include window switches for a burglar-alarm system or the resistance change of a thermistor for a thermostat control system. The applications are endless.

There are basically 2 types of joysticks available. The first is the 2-axis switch type, such as the one used by Atari® video games. This joystick actually consists of 4 single-pole switches. When the stick is moved away from the center, the switch representing that direction is closed. This movement only gives an all-the-way-off or all-the-way-on action but, with proper software, can be very effective, as the Atari games have proven. The second and more sophisticated type of joystick is the analog type, which is found on the Apple and Radio Shack computers. These joysticks are actually 100K potentiometers. That variability allows the computer to detect an almost infinite variety of settings, not just an off or on condition. We call this circuitry an *analog* sensor, since the computer arrives at a number that is analogous to the setting of the stick. Both types will be described here in detail.

Switch-operated joysticks

As one would imagine, the switch-type joysticks are the simplest to interface. For example, it would be possible to build a parallel input port and sense the switch states as shown in Figure 7-1. In this arrangement, the inputs to 5 3-state buffers are held high by pull-up resistors. When a switch is closed, the input goes to a logic low state. The condition is detected by a PEEK at the address decoded by the 74LS138 decoder. The decimal values of the addresses are indicated in the schematic, provided you use Pin 9 of the 74LS138 ROM decoder as the device strobe for this circuit. A switch-open condition will return a 255 and a switch-closed condition will return a 127 with the PEEK.

In a recent *Syntax* article, "Adding a Joystick to ZX80/81" (June 1982), Dave Straub presented a much simpler method of interfacing a switch-type joystick; we would like to include it here. The keyboards for Sinclair computers are of the matrix type. Address lines go horizontally across the keyboard and inputs to the data lines pass in the vertical direction. A given row can be selected by reading an address code that brings only 1 address line low. Any key closure in that row will cause the data line crossing the selected address row at that point to go low. That lowering, in turn, sets the corresponding bit to 0 on the byte that was loaded into the accumulator. The software is continuously scanning all the key-

FIGURE 7-1
Joysticks connected via a parallel input port

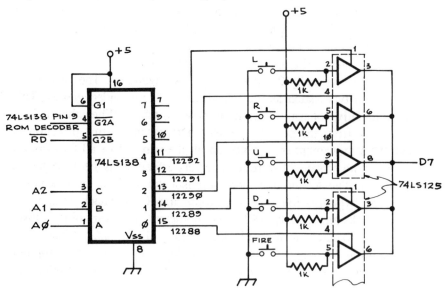

board rows looking for a switch closure. It would be a simple matter to add the joystick so that it simulated a key press. Figures 7-2 and 7-3 show an Atari 2-axis stick with the fire button attached to the ZX80 and the ZX81, respectively. You will have to use an ohm meter to locate the common and the other 5 wires coming out of the joystick. It would be ideal if the 4 directional switches could be wired up to simulate closure of the keys 5 through 8, since these keys have the cursor mnemonics on them; unfortunately the wiring of the keyboard matrix makes this wiring impossible since there is only one common line from the switches. One word of caution at this point: if you bought your ZX81 or Timex assembled, adding connections to the main board as described here will void your warranty. If you assembled your computer yourself, it won't make any difference. Make your solder connections very neatly and be careful not to allow any shorts with bare wires or any solder bridges. When connections are made, turn on

FIGURE 7-2
Joysticks added via the ZX81 keyboard. Avoid solder bridges when making these connections. The symbols beside the switches indicate the key to which each switch corresponds. The number refers to the LAST-K code.

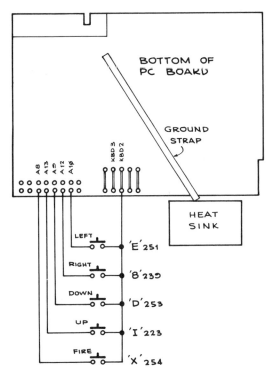

FIGURE 7-3
Joysticks connected via the ZX80 keyboard. The symbols refer to the key to which each switch corresponds. If an 8K ROM is included, the LAST-K codes will be the same as in Figure 7-2.

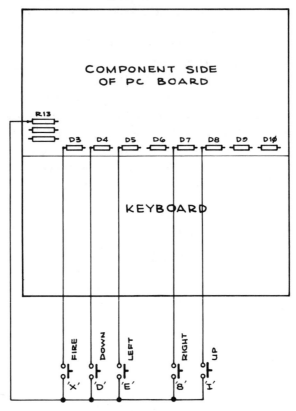

the monitor and apply power to the computer. The cursor should come up immediately. If it does not, turn the power off and locate the problem. You probably have a short. Once you have a cursor, push the joystick to the right. An 8 should appear; push it to the left; a REM should appear. Pushing it up should yield an I, and pushing it down should yield a D. Pushing the fire button should produce an X. If you have a machine with a 4K ROM, you will see SAVE instead of the REM.

Programming switch-type joysticks

There are 2 ways to program the switch-type joystick just described. The most obvious way to detect a switch closure is with the INKEY$ Command. For example:

IF INKEY$ = "E" THEN PRINT "LEFT"

will print the message LEFT if the joystick was moved to the left at the time the command was executed. Unfortunately INKEY$ is a rather slow instruction and can waste valuable time if it is in a complex loop. A quicker way to detect a switch closure is to PEEK at LAST-K at 16421. This command tells the last key pressed, but the key code is in relation to the matrix and not in Sinclair's alphanumeric code. The following table tells what the codes are for the 8K ROM.

FUNCTION	KEY	LAST-K CODE
LEFT	E	251
RIGHT	8	239
DOWN	D	253
UP	I	223
FIRE	X	254

Thus the preceding command could also be written

IF PEEK 16421 = 251 THEN PRINT "LEFT"

This change would greatly speed up execution time. The following is a simple program using the joystick to draw figures on the screen. It is based on William Wentz's Video artist program ("Video Artist—8K/2K" *Syntax*, March, 1982).

```
 2 LET P = 16421
 5 LET A = 1
10 LET X = A
12 LET Y = A
14 LET P = A
16 PRINT "ENTER TITLE"
20 INPUT A$
25 CLS
30 PLOT X, Y
40 UNPLOT X, Y
45 IF P = A, THEN PLOT X, Y
50 IF PEEK P = 251 THEN LET X = ABS (X−A)
60 IF PEEK P = 253 THEN LET Y = ABS (Y−A)
70 IF PEEK P = 223 THEN LET Y = Y+A
80 IF PEEK P = 239 THEN LET X = X+A
```

```
90 IF PEEK P = 254 THEN LET P = P * −1
110 IF INKEY$ = "S" THEN SAVE A$
120 IF X>40 THEN LET X = X−A
130 IF Y>40 THEN LET Y = Y−A
140 GO TO 30
```

Moving the joystick will direct the cursor around the screen. Each time the fire button is pushed, the program will change from the save-trace mode to the erase-trace mode. When the figure is drawn the way you like it, start the tape recorder and push the S key. The picture and program will be saved on tape. This program will run in 1K of RAM with the 8K ROM. If you want to run it on an upgraded ZX80, you will have to add:

```
46 PAUSE 20
```

so that you can see the figure as you draw it.

Analog joysticks

There are several ways to add an analog joystick to your machine. One way would be through an analog-to-digital converter, as was described in Chapter 6. If you have already built the analog-to-digital converter, then by all means simply add the joysticks as shown in Figure 7-4. Up to 16 potentiometers can be added with the ADC0816 chip. But let's assume you have not built the ADC0816 analog-to-digital converter. What is the simplest and least expensive method for enabling the computer to detect a resistance change? The most common solution to this problem has been the use of a 555 or 556 timer chip used in a 1-shot mode. In this mode the output of the timer goes high upon triggering, stays high for a preset time period, and then returns to the low state. The time period is determined by the RC time constant of the external resistor and capacitor. If the resistance in this circuit changes, then so will the delay time. All that remains is for the computer to trigger the 1 shot and determine the delay period. The delay will be proportional to the resistance in the RC circuit. That resistance, of course, will be the variable resistor in the joystick. The 555 and 556 are identical chips, except that the 556 is a dual circuit and essentially contains 2 555s. Figure 7-5 shows an interface on the expansion board that provides for 2 such variable resistors and uses a 556 chip. It could be expanded to provide for up to 8 such resistors by using more 555s and 74LS126 3-state buffers. In this arrangement, a POKE to address $3000 (12288 decimal) will pass the data-transfer strobe directly to the trigger inputs of the timer

FIGURE 7-4
Joysticks connected with the ADC described in Chapter
6. Up to 16 joysticks can be added this way.

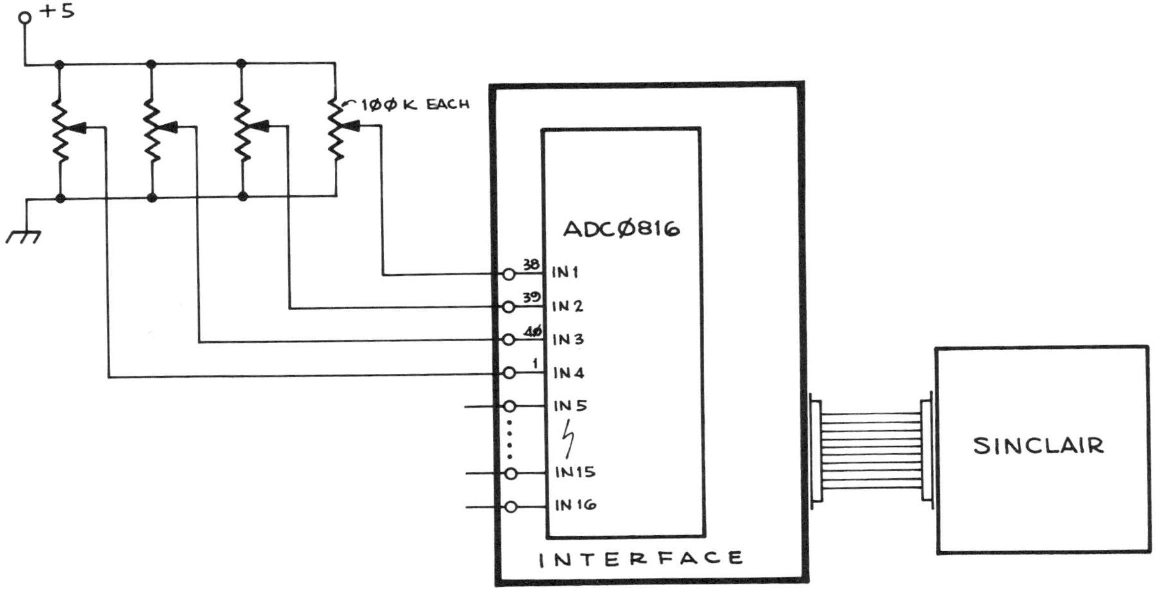

FIGURE 7-5

Joysticks using the 556. Note that 2 555s can be
substituted for the 556. The numbers in parentheses
refer to 555 pins. The 100K variable resistors are the
joystick potentiometers.

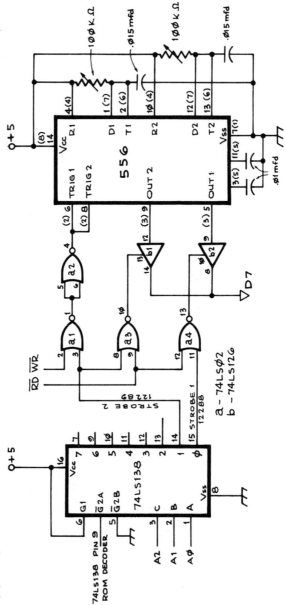

74LS27

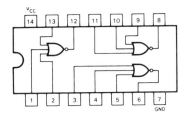

chips. The outputs of the timers go to 3-state buffers on data line 7. A PEEK at 11288 decimal will reveal the state of timer 1, and a PEEK at 12289 will sample timer 2. If the timer is active, a 255 will be returned, and if it has returned to the quiescent state, a 127 will be read.

Checkout procedure for analog joysticks

After you have built the preceding circuit, insert all ICs except for the 74LS126 3-state buffer. Double check for errors in wiring, since they could damage the computer. When you are satisfied that all is okay, plug the expansion board into the computer, turn on the monitor, and, after it has warmed up, apply power to the computer. If a cursor does not appear immediately, unplug the power and locate the problem. Look for shorted address or data lines or shorts across the power. Be sure that there are +5 volts on the board when the computer is plugged in.

Assuming that you now have a cursor, take a logic probe and put it on Pin 6 and 8 of the 556. Both these pins should show a logic high. Similarly the command

POKE 12288,0

should cause a pulse on these pins. If not, check the 74LS02 for wiring errors. Now put the probe on Pin 5 of the 556. This pin should be low. The command

POKE 12288,0

should cause a pulse here as well. The same result should be seen on Pin 9 of the 556. This pulse means that the 1 shot is working. Next put the probe

91

on Pin 13 of the socket for the 74LS126 tristate buffer. It should be at a logic low.

PRINT PEEK 12288

should result in a pulse. If not, check the wiring of the 74LS02. Finally put the probe on Pin 10 of the 74LS126 socket. It again should register a logic low.

PRINT PEEK 12289

should generate a pulse here. Hint: failure to wire the power and ground pins is the most common cause of nonfunctioning circuits. If all these tests check out, unplug the computer, insert the 74LS126 into its socket, and turn the power back on.

PRINT PEEK 12288, PEEK 12289

should return two 127s.

Programming the joysticks (8K ROM users)

The output pulse from the joysticks ranges from about 0.5 to 5 ms in duration. This rate is too fast for BASIC to count. Therefore it will be necessary to use a short machine-language program to control the joysticks. The program appears in Listing 7-1. If you don't understand it, don't worry; it isn't necessary. To use the program, it is first necessary to store it in a safe place. We will do this in a REM statement in line 1 of the program. This is a safe place because we know that it will start at 16514. Since it is on line 1, nothing can be placed ahead of it to move it from that location. Now enter the following program:

```
1 REM 012345678901234567890123456789
12 LET CS = 0
13 FOR I = 16514 to 16539
14 PRINT AT 0,20;I
15 INPUT N
16 POKE I,N
17 LET CS = CS+N
18 NEXT I
19 PRINT CS
```

LISTING 7-1
Machine-language joystick program for the 8K ROM

```
        *   JOYSTICK PROGRAM FOR 8K ROM
        *
        *   EQUATES:
        *   FRAMES  .EQ   $4034
        *   JOYSTX  .EQ   $3000
        *
  40A6  0100    ENTRY:  LD BC, $0000   ;  CLEAR BC
  40A9  320030          LD JOYSTX, A   ;  START ONE SHOT
  40AC  3A0030  LOOP:   LD A, JOYSTX   ;  PUT FLAG IN A
  40AF  03              INC BC         ;  LOOP COUNTER
  40B0  07              RLC A          ;  SHIFT FLAG INTO CARRY
  40B1  38 F9           JRC LOOP       ;  LOOP IF NOT TIME OUT
  40B3  C9              RET            ;  TIME OUT, RETURN
        *
        *   RETRACE SYNCHRONIZATION FOR SLOW MODE
        *
  40B4  3A3440  ENTR :  LD A, FRAMES   ;  GET FRAME COUNTER
  40B7  47              LD B, A        ;  PUT IN B
  40B8  3A3440  AGAIN:  LD A, FRAMES   ;  GET FRAMES AGAIN
  40BB  B8              CP B           ;  HAS FRAMES CHANGED?
  40BC  28FA            JRZ AGAIN      ;  NO, TRY AGAIN
  40BE  18E6            JR ENTRY 1     ;  YES START ONE SHOT
        *
        *   COUNT IN BC REGISTER ON RETURN
        *
```

This program will ask for the consecutive bytes of machine code and POKE them in sequence in the REM statement in line 1.

CS is a running sum of these codes and will yield a checksum that will help detect any entry errors. Start the program and enter the following series of numbers in order:

1, 0, 0, 50, 0, 48, 58, 0, 48, 3, 7, 56, 249, 201, 58, 52, 64, 71, 58, 52, 64, 184, 40, 250, 24, 230

After the 230 is entered, the computer should print the checksum value 1868 on the screen. If a number other than that appears, you made a mistake in entering the list and you should try again. Once you have successfully entered the list of numbers, relist the program. Notice that the sequence after the REM has been replaced by what appears to be garbage. It is really the machine-language program stored in the BASIC program buffer following the REM and the machine's attempt to display it as alphanumeric characters. Add the following lines:

```
  5 GOTO 100
  100 PRINT USR 16528; " " '
  110 GOTO 100
```

At this point, it would be a good idea to save the program on tape, since a crash in a machine-language program is often unrecoverable. Put the computer in SLOW mode and start it (if you are using an upgraded ZX80, change the 16528 to 16514 in line 100 and add 105 PAUSE 20, since that machine does not support the slow mode).

Numbers should appear on the screen as you change the position of Control 1. These numbers should range from about 10 with the control in one extreme to about 120 at the other extreme. If the numbers exceed 120, then the capacitor is too large. If they are much smaller than 120, increase the size of the capacitor. If they don't change, you have a hardware problem with the timer.

Stop the program and enter the following immediate-mode command:

POKE 16521,1

Now restart the program; the numbers on the screen should be affected by changing Control 2.

Lines 12–18 were only needed to enter the program behind the REM statement and can now be deleted. Before we go on, however, it will be necessary to explain a little about the machine-language routine. The Z80 is time shared in the Sinclair computer. In the slow mode, it refreshes the screen by generating a video signal. Only during the vertical-retrace time does it do any BASIC calculations. Thus most of the time it is not available to measure the pulse duration; it's busy displaying the screen. This problem is overcome by the code starting at 16528. The program waits until the very start of a retrace cycle by detecting a change in the FRAMES counter. It then triggers the timer chip, which is designed to time out before the retrace cycle is finished. Thus the choice of 100K ohms and .015 μF is critical in the circuit. If your potentiometer is something different from 100K ohms, choose a capacitor such that

$$C = 1.5/R$$

where C is in microfarads and R is in kilohms.

In the FAST mode the computer does not try to refresh the screen, so it is available for BASIC calculations all the time. Furthermore, in this mode, it does not increment the FRAMES counter. If you do a USR 16528 in the FAST mode, it will get hung up waiting for the FRAMES counter to change. In the FAST mode you must enter the routine at 16514, thus bypassing the synchronization step. *If you have the upgraded ZX80 (8K ROM)*, you only have the FAST mode available to you. That is why you should never try to enter the program with a USR 16528 in that particular machine.

The following is a program that uses a 2-axis joystick to direct the cursor around the screen. When the program is first started in the SLOW mode, you must enter a title from the keyboard. Hitting the "P" will cause the cursor to be permanently plotted on the screen. The "U" key will cause it to go into the unplot mode. When your picture is finished, start the tape recorder in the record mode and hit the "S" key. The program and the picture will be saved.

```
  1 REM
 80 INPUT A$
 90 LET Z=1
100 POKE 16521,0
110 LET X=(USR 16528)/2
120 POKE 1-521,1
130 LET Y=(USR 16526)/3
140 PLOT X,Y
145 UNPLOT X,Y
150 IF X=0 THEN PLOT X,Y
155 IF INKEY$="S" THEN SAVE A$
160 IF INKEY$="P" THEN LET Z=0
165 IF INKEY$="U" THEN LET Z=1
170 GOTO 100
```

Programming the joysticks (4K ROM users)

The joystick interface works on the Sinclair computers with the 4K ROM as well. The program to run the joystick is a little different, however. The USR command in the 8K machines assumes the numerical value from the subroutine to be returned in the B-C registers of the Z80. The 4K machines require the answer to be returned in the H-L register pair. For this reason,

LISTING 7-2
Machine-language joystick program for the 4K ROM

```
     *   JOYSTICK PROGRAM FOR 4K ROM
     *
     *   EQUATES:
     *   JOYSTICK . EQ    $3000
     *
     *
  402B   210000    ENTRY:  LD HL, $0000   ;   CLEAR HL
  402E   320032            LD JOYSTX, A   ;   START ONE SHOT
  403I   3A0032    LOOP:   LD A, JOYSTX   ;   PUT FLAG IN A
  4034   23                INC HL         ;   INCREMENT HL
  4035   07                RLC A          ;   ROTATE FLAG INTO CARRY
  4036   38F9              JRC LOOP       ;   LOOP IF NOT TIME OUT
  4038   C9                RET            ;   TIME OUT, RETURN
     *
     *   COUNT IS IN HL FOR THE 4K VERSION
     *
```

the first and tenth bytes must be changed. Byte 1 goes from a 1 (LD BC, NN) to a 42 (LD HL, NN). Byte 10 is changed from a 3 (INC BC) to a 43 (INC HL). Also the 4K systems do not support the SLOW mode of operation, so there is no reason to synchronize the FRAMES. For this reason, the last half of the preceding routine is not required. Finally the starting location of the program buffer is different in the 4K systems. The first byte following a 1 REM statement is 16427 in that system as opposed to 16514 in the 8K system.

The set-up program for the 4K machine-language routine appears as follows:

```
1 REM 1234567890123456
10 LET CS=0
20 FOR I=16427 to 16440
30 PRINT I
40 INPUT N
50 POKE I,N
60 CLS
70 LET CS=CS+N
80 NEXT I
90 PRINT CS
```

After entering this program, run it and enter the following series of numbers: 33, 0, 0, 50, 0, 48, 58, 0, 48, 35, 7, 56, 249, 201.

If the numbers were entered correctly, a checksum of 785 will appear on the screen. Press the enter key and get a program listing. Note that the numbers following the REM statement have been replaced with garbage. This is the machine-language program behind the REM statement. Now add the following lines and run the program:

```
5 GOTO 100
100 PRINT ABS (USR(16427)); " ";
110 GOTO 100
```

The screen should fill with numbers proportional to the setting of the Channel 1 joystick. Change the setting of the stick and rerun the program. Once the machine code has been inserted in the REM statement, lines 10 through 90 may be deleted. When you save the program on tape, the machine code will be preserved and need never be entered again as long as the REM statement in line 1 is not altered.

8

MEMORY
EXPANSION

You may wish to expand the memory of your Sinclair computer using 1 or more of the following modes:

1. ROM for permanent machine-language storage
2. RAM protected from BASIC for temporary storage of data or machine-language programs
3. RAM for minor expansion of BASIC program space

We will cover each of these expansion modes in this chapter. You will note that we have not included major BASIC RAM expansion because the most cost-effective method is the addition of the Sinclair 16K RAM expansion pack, which can be plugged directly into your Sinclair or into the bus expansion socket on the expansion board as described in Chapter 3. All 3 of our memory expansion alternates can be built on this expansion board.

Adding a 2716 ROM

We must assume that you programmed a 350 nanosecond 5-volt 2716 ROM with the exact code you want to run and that you want to wire this ROM into your expansion board, which already contains the ROM decoder described in Chapter 3.

Fix a 24-pin wire-wrap socket to your board and wire according to Figure 8-1. Connect 5-volt power and ground to the appropriate pins, the 8 data lines D0–D7, and the lower 11 address lines A0–A10. As a bonus, we suggest you wire Pin 21 to the $\overline{WR}$ signal, so that the same socket can be used for a 6116 RAM if your requirements change. Alternatively you can tie Pin 21 to +5 volts.

Pin 18 is the data-transfer strobe for the ROM. How it is connected is determined by where in the system memory space you wish the ROM to be active. You may use any one of the unused outputs of the ROM decoder (Chapter 3). For example, if your ROM program is to occupy the 2K block $3800–$3FFF, wire your ROM Pin 18 to Pin 7 of the 74LS138 ROM decoder.

You may verify your work by PEEKing at a few of the new ROM's addresses. These PEEKs should agree with the bytes you have pro-grammed into the ROM. If your Sinclair is dead with the ROM plugged in, the cause could be:

1. A wiring error
2. Overloading of a signal line by having too many devices connected.

FIGURE 8-1
2716 ROM schematic. Note that this circuit can be used for RAM chips (6116 or 2016).

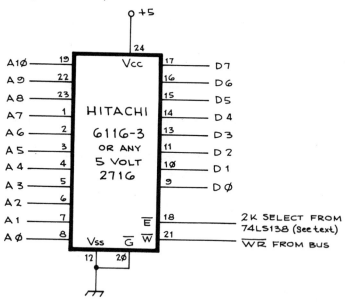

If all the PEEKs at the ROM are 255s ($FF), the ROM is not being activated. Recalculate the PEEK addresses and check the wiring.

We hope that a few avid Z80 machine-language programmers will develop neat programs for your Sinclair and will offer them in preprogrammed ROMs for your expansion board. How about machine-language monitors, assemblers, text editors, games, terminal programs, ham programs, and so on? There are enough Sinclairs out there to make an attractive market for some enterprising programmers.

Protected RAM

When your Sinclair powers up, it checks to determine how much memory has been connected. It does this by storing $02 in every address from $7FFF down to $4000. It then starts upward at $4000 and decrements each byte twice, and when a number not 0 is found, it assumes that the high end of memory is located. With the 8K Sinclair ROM, this value is stored at $4004 and $4005 (decimal 16388 and 16389), with the low-order byte first. In fact, you can PEEK at 16389 for quick verification of memory validity. It should be

PEEK 16389 = 64 + 4 * N

where N is the number of K of good memory.

As a result of the memory test, any memory in the range $4000 to $7FFF is set to zero. This change occurs at power-up or if the reset button, which you may have installed on your expansion board, is pressed. However any new RAM located outside this address range will be unaffected by this initialization procedure. A convenient place for this memory is the space formerly occupied by a ROM image—that is, $2000–$3FFF. You may select 1 of the 2K blocks available at the ROM decoder for your protected expansion RAM.

The circuit of Figure 8-1 can be used to handle a 2Kx8 6116 RAM chip. It is probably the hottest-selling RAM chip on the market as of this writing, since it is pin-compatible with the popular 2716 ROM and provides a great deal of RAM in a single package. It is CMOS and thus adds very little loading to signal lines and power supplies.

Expanding BASIC's RAM

There are certain constraints that must be observed if you are adding RAM to expand the space available for BASIC programs. The first of these is that additional RAM must be in address spaces that are contiguous with the original RAM; that is, if you have 1K on the Sinclair board, it will occupy $4000–$43FF and the expansion RAM must then start at $4400. Further addition of RAM must follow this same rule, as BASIC will assume the first nonfunctional byte of memory it encounters on power-up to be the top of RAM.

Another requirement is that an outboard RAM decoder must be installed in order to remove some of the original RAM images arising from incomplete decoding inside the Sinclair. Figure 8-2 shows how to implement the expansion-board RAM decoder, using a 74LS138 similar to the

FIGURE 8-2
RAM decoder. Circuit keeps original RAM active and allows address space for expansion.

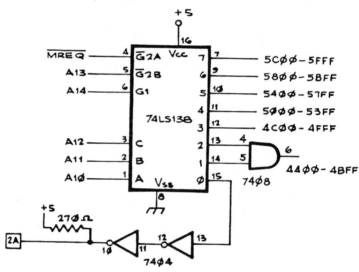

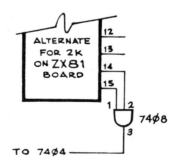

RAM decoder described in Chapter 3. It creates outputs representing 1K each.

The third constraint is that for the Sinclair's display to work, a RAM image *must* exist 32K higher. To accomplish this result, we simply do not connect address line A15 to the RAM decoder.

For example, a 2K expansion can be made to BASIC's RAM using the 6116 circuit shown in Figure 8-1. First determine whether you have 1K (Sinclair ZX81) or 2K (Timex 1000) of RAM in your machine. Take the next 2 adjacent unused outputs of the 74LS138 decoder—for example, Pins 14 and 13 if you have a 1K unit—and route them to Pin 18 of the 6116 through a 7408 AND gate as shown in Figure 8-2. For a 2K Sinclair, use Pins 13 and 12 of the 74LS138. Note also that an additional AND gate is required on Pins 15 and 16 of the 74LS138 to control the onboard RAM in the 2K Sinclair (see insert of Figure 8-2). The power and ground pins on the 7408 are 14 and 7 respectively.

You may also add pairs of 2114 1Kx4 RAM chips for expansion. It takes 4 chips to provide 2K equivalent to a single 6116, and the 18-pin wire-wrap sockets can be hard to locate. Since most people would much rather wire 24 pins than 18×4 or 72 pins to obtain 2K of expansion, the 2114s are not the best choice, but they will work. The cost of chips and sockets is roughly equal. All except the 4 data pins and the chip-select pins of the 2114s are wired in parallel. Half the data lines go to one chip and the other half to the other chip of a pair. The chip selects of any pair go to the desired pin of the RAM decoder. These connections are shown in Figure 8-3.

When you have added the RAM decoder, power-up without the RAM chips. If the Sinclair does not work, you have a wiring error or a faulty 74LS138.

Plug in the RAM chips with the power off and restart. A

PRINT PEEK 16389

should give you a value according to the equation above under "Protected RAM." (Remember that start-up given on p. 99 tested this RAM for you and saved the ending value at 16388 and 16389.) If you do not get the proper value, check your wiring, your cable continuity, and the appropriateness of the select lines from the 74LS138.

Unlike memory-expansion packs, the preceding RAM expansions retain the operation of the original 1K or 2K of RAM on the Sinclair board. The 16K pack ties the $\overline{\text{RAMCS}}$ line high to 5 volts and thus disables onboard RAM. The 16K pack is thus not compatible with the BASIC

FIGURE 8-3
2114 RAM expansion. Each 1K of expansion requires 1
pair of 2114s.

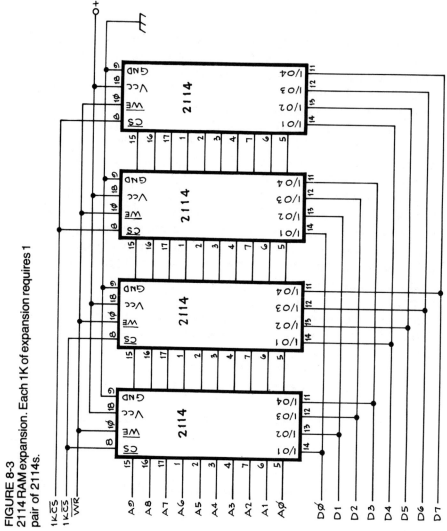

program RAM expansion, but it is compatible with any protected RAM addition.

RAM testing

You may test any of the RAM additions with the following program:

PROGRAM	COMMENTS
10 FAST	
20 LET BEGADR = 4*4096+4*256	Hex 4400
30 LET RAMSIZE = 2*1024	Ram is 2K
40 FOR I = BEGADR to BEGADR+RAMSIZE+1	
50 LET C = 255−PEEK I	Flip all bits
60 POKE I, C	
70 IF PEEK I <> C THEN PRINT I−BEGADR	
80 NEXT I	
90 SLOW	

You will wish to change line 20 to accord with the beginning address of your expansion RAM and line 30 to reflect its size. The relative location of bad bytes will appear on the screen. We have rigged the program to show the 2 bad bytes at locations following good RAM. If the RAM is good, the screen will show the following for 1K and 2K expansion:

1K	2K
1024	2048
1025	2049

If a few more numbers appear, the RAM chips are probably faulty. The program takes about 22 seconds per K of RAM, so be patient! If every byte is bad, the program or wiring should be suspect.

The program flips every bit in the RAM and verifies that 0s became 1s and 1s became 0s.

9

INTERFACING
PRINTERS

Hard copy from a printer is useful for producing a report of results. Furthermore it is the only way to make a permanent listing of your programs. If your program contains bugs, studying a printed listing will often give quicker solutions and allow quicker de-bugging. In this chapter we will describe two printer interfaces that can be used with your Sinclair computer. Either one can be built on the basic expansion board described in Chapter 2. There are many serial printers available, but the most popular is the surplus Model 33 Teletype, which is available in the $150–$300 range. Remember, however, that this interface will also work even with the Cadillacs of serial printers. Imagine the $100 Sinclair hooked to a $3000 printer! If you have such a printer available, it will work.

Serial printers

What is meant by "serial"? It simply means that data representing characters are transmitted over a pair of wires—one carrying the signal and the other providing a return path. In order to send the information for 1 character, a series of electrical events is sent over the wires; each element of the series is separated by a fixed time interval, which in practical application may range from 1/50 second down to 1/19200 second. The rate of

FIGURE 9-1

Serial printer schematic. The 6850 ACIA is used to
convert parallel computer data to serial printer data.

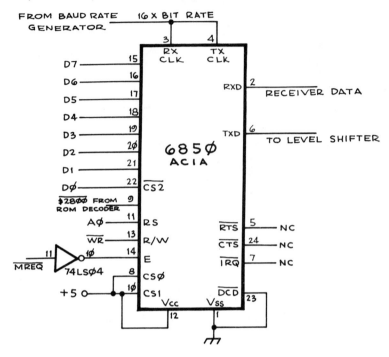

sending these bits of information is commonly called the *baud rate*; our
range is 50 baud through 19200 baud.

The electrical events over the pair of wires can be a series of voltage
changes (TTL or RS232 levels) or a series of interruptions to current flow
(current loop, either 20 milliampere (ma) or 60 ma). Most common serial
computer peripherals use RS232 voltage levels, roughly defined as a swing
from -12 volts to $+12$ volts. The Model 33 Teletype uses the 20 ma.
current-loop method, which allows an entire network of teletypes to be
connected in series, all printing the same message.

We will be dealing with asynchronous signals, which in our case
means that a character will be sent whenever the transmitting device is
ready and has a character to print. This method does not mean that the bit
rate within a character can change. On the contrary, both the transmitting
device and the receiving device must be set to the same baud rate. Many
printers have adjustable baud rates, but the Model 33 Teletype, for example, is fixed at 110 baud because it is primarily a mechanical device with a
fixed speed of rotation.

There are several alternate bit codes for characters. We will deal only with the American Standard for Computer Information Interchange (AS-CII) code, which is used in most modern computers and peripherals. Your Sinclair is an exception, in that it internally uses its own code for characters; but as you will see, the Sinclair can make the conversion for us. The ASCII code is shown in Table 9-1. The coding used by the Sinclair is given on page 7.

TABLE 9-1: The ASCII Code

DECIMAL	HEX	ASCII	DECIMAL	HEX	ASCII
32	20	SPACE	62	3E	>
33	21	!	63	3F	?
34	22	"	64	40	@
35	23	#	65	41	A
36	24	$	66	42	B
37	25	%	67	43	C
38	26	&	68	44	D
39	27	'	69	45	E
40	28	(	70	46	F
41	29	)	71	47	G
42	2A	*	72	48	H
43	2B	+	73	49	I
44	2C	,	74	4A	J
45	2D	-	75	4B	K
46	2E	.	76	4C	L
47	2F	/	77	4D	M
48	30	0	78	4E	N
49	31	1	79	4F	O
50	32	2	80	50	P
51	33	3	81	51	Q
52	34	4	82	52	R
53	35	5	83	53	S
54	36	6	84	54	T
55	37	7	85	55	U
56	38	8	86	56	V
57	39	9	87	57	W
58	3A	:	88	58	X
59	3B	;	89	59	Y
60	3C	<	90	5A	Z
61	3D	=			

A serial ASCII character can be represented by the following diagram:

FIGURE 9-2
Character format

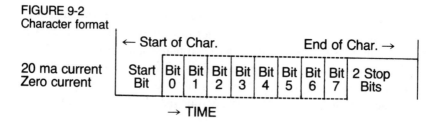

← Start of Char.									End of Char. →

20 ma current
Zero current

| Start Bit | Bit 0 | Bit 1 | Bit 2 | Bit 3 | Bit 4 | Bit 5 | Bit 6 | Bit 7 | 2 Stop Bits |

→ TIME

A character begins when current is interrupted, or voltage goes to its active state, for 1 bit-time; this interval is called a *start bit*. It is followed by current–no current intervals (currents are often referred to as *marks*, and no current is referred to as a *space*) representing the 8 bits of a character starting with bit 0. At the end of our character are shown 2 *stop bits*, where the current or voltage is returned to the normally idle state. The next character can immediately follow these stop bits, or there may be an indefinite gap, from milliseconds to months. Now that's asynchronous!

This is only 1 of several possible character formats, but we will use it, since it is the most compatible format. There can be these variations:

1. 7 instead of 8 data bits
2. 1 instead of 2 stop bits
3. An extra *parity* or check bit after the last data bit

Our 8-bit, 2-stop-bit, nonparity format actually requires 11 bit-times per character. If we operate at 110 baud, then the maximum transmission rate is 110/11 or 10 characters per second. At the fast end of the range, 19200 baud would allow 1745 characters per second. A common misconception is that a higher baud rate will always result in a higher character-transmission rate; this result is true only if the transmitting device is capable of generating characters at a rate greater than that dictated by the baud rate.

Selection of the hardware

It is possible to transmit serially from a computer via a single-bit output port. To accomplish this transmission our computer software would output a start bit, delay in software for 1 bit-time, output each data bit in succession with appropriate delays, and output a stop bit with a 2-bit-time delay. Many single-board computers use this software method of character transmission.

In our case, it is much more convenient to use a hardware device that can be fed characters over the computer's normal parallel data bus and to

LISTING 9-1
Printer ROM Routine

```
0001 * ASCII SERIAL/PARALLEL PRINTER DRIVER
0002 *
0003 *----------------------------------
0004 * EQUATES:
0005 STATUS .EQ $2800     ACIA STATUS REGISTER
0006 CONTRL .EQ $2800     ACIA CONTROL REGISTER
0007 DATARG .EQ $2801     ACIA DATA REGISTER
0008 DFILE  .EQ $400C     DISPLAY FILE POINTER
0009 FLAG   .EQ $407B     ACIA INIT. FLAG, 00 = NOT INIT.
0010 *----------------------------------
0011 *
0012 * PRINTS A SPACE FOR GRAPHICS AND
0013 * INVERTED CHARACTERS. USES $407B AS
0014 * FLAG FOR ACIA INITIALLIZATION.
0015 *
0016 * ROUTINE WORKS WITH BOTH SERIAL AND
0017 * PARALLEL PRINTERS, WITH PROPER HARDWARE
0018 *
0019 * ORIGINAL ROM CODE PLACED AT $0800-0850 AND
0020 * AT $08DE-08FF.
0021 *
0022 *----------------------------------
0023 * PRTCHR MUST BE AT $0851
0024 0851 F5         PRTCHR PUSH AF        ; SAVE THE CHARACTER
0025 0852 3A 7B 40          LD A,(FLAG)     ; TEST ACIA INIT.
0026 0855 A7               AND A           ; IS IT ZERO?
0027 0856 20 0D            JR NZ,SKIP      ; JUMP IF INITIALIZED
0028 0858 3E 13            LD A,$13        ; ACIA RESET BYTE
0029 085A 32 7B 40         LD (FLAG),A     ; NON-ZERO TO FLAG
0030 085D 32 00 28         LD (CONTRL),A; RESET ACIA
0031 0860 3E 11            LD A,$11        ; ACIA SETUP BYTE
0032 0862 32 00 28         LD (CONTRL),A; TO ACIA CONTROL REG
0033 0865 F1         SKIP  POP AF          ; GET CHAR. BACK
0034 0866 18 25            JR CONTIN       ; SKIP OVER COPY AND CRET
0035 0868 00               NOP
0036 *----------------------------------
0037 * COPY MUST BE AT $0869
0038 0869 16 16      COPY   LD D,$16       ; 24 LINES
0039 086B 2A 0C 40          LD HL,(DFILE); GET FILE POINTER
0040 086E 23         COPY1  INC HL         ; NEXT BYTE
0041 086F 18 43             JR COPY2       ; SKIP TO PATCH
0042 *----------------------------------
0043 * CRET MUST BE AT $0871
0044 0871 06 05      CRET   LD B,5         ; DO 5 CRET'S
0045 0873 3E 0D      CRET1  LD A,$0D       ; GET ASCII CRET
0046 0875 CD 80 08          CALL UART      ; OUTPUT IT
0047 0878 10 F9             DJNZ CRET1     ; LOOP UNTIL DONE
0048 087A 3E 0A             LD A,$0A       ; GET ASCII LINEFEED
0049 087C 18 02             JR UART        ; EXIT VIA UART
0050 087E 3E 20      SPACE  LD A,$20       ; GET ASCII SPACE
0051 0880 F5         UART   PUSH AF        ; SAVE THE CHAR.
0052 0881 3A 00 28   UART1  LD A,(STATUS); GET ACIA STATUS
0053 0884 E6 02             AND $02        ; ISOLATE XMT BIT
0054 0886 28 F9             JR Z UART1     ; LOOP WHILE BUSY
0055 0888 F1               POP AF          ; GET CHAR BACK
0056 0889 32 01 28         LD (DATARG),A; CHAR TO ACIA
0057 088C C9               RET
0058 *----------------------------------
0059 * CONTINUATION OF PRTCHR ROUTINE
0060 088D FE 76      CONTIN CP $76         ; IS IT CRET?
0061 088F 28 E0             JR Z CRET      ; IF SO, GO DO IT
0062 0891 A7               AND A           ; TEST FOR SPACE (00)
0063 0892 28 EA            JR Z SPACE      ; IF SPACE, GO THERE
0064 0894 FE 40            CP $40          ; GREATER THAN Z?
0065 0896 30 E6            JR NC SPACE     ; DO SPACE
0066 0898 FE 26            CP $26          ; LESS THAN A?
0067 089A 38 04            JR C CONT2      ; IF SO, TEST MORE
0068 089C C6 1B            ADD A,$1B       ; GET ASCII LETTER
```

```
0069 089E 18 E0            JR UART        ; OUTPUT LETTER
0070 08A0 FE 1C    CONT2   CP #1C         ; LESS THAN 0?
0071 08A2 38 04            JR C CONT3     ; IF SO, TEST MORE
0072 08A4 C6 14            ADD A,#14      ; CONVERT TO ASCII NUMBER
0073 08A6 18 D8            JR UART        ; OUTPUT NUMBER
0074 08A8 FE 0B    CONT3   CP #0B         ; BELOW PUNCTUATION?
0075 08AA 38 D2            JR C SPACE     ; DO SPACE
0076 08AC 21 C2 08         LD HL,TABLE-11 ; TABLE @ #08CD
0077 08AF 85               ADD A,L        ; CALCULATE ADDRESS
0078 08B0 6F               LD L,A         ; ADDR TO HL
0079 08B1 7E               LD A,(HL)      ; GET ASCII PUNCT.
0080 08B2 18 CC            JR UART        ; OUTPUT IT
0081 *---------------------------------
0082 * PATCH FOR COPY ROUTINE
0083 08B4 7E       COPY2   LD A,(HL)      ; GET DISPLAY CHAR.
0084 08B5 E5               PUSH HL        ; SAVE POINTER
0085 08B6 CD 51 08         CALL PRTCHR    ; PRINT A CHAR.
0086 08B9 E1               POP HL         ; GET POINTER
0087 08BA FE 0A            CP #0A         ; IS IT LINEFEED?
0088 08BC 20 B0            JR NZ COPY1    ; BACK IF NOT
0089 08BE 15               DEC D          ; DECR LINE COUNT
0090 08BF 20 AD            JR NZ COPY1
0091 08C1 C9               RET
0092 *---------------------------------
0093 * SPACE FOR MORE HACKING
0094 08C2 00 00 00
0095 08C5 00 00 00
0096 08C8 00 00 00
0097 08CB 00 00            ELEVEN NOP'S
0098 *---------------------------------
0099 * SINCLAIR-TO-ASCII PUNCTUATION CONVERSION TABLE
0100 *
0101 08CD 22 23 24 TABLE   .AS "#$:?()><=+-*/;,.
0102 08D0 3A 3F 28
0103 08D3 29 3E 3C
0104 08D6 3D 2B 2D
0105 08D9 2A 2F 3B
0106 08DC 2C 2E
0107 *---------------------------------
0108 * ORIGINAL CODE CONTINUES HERE
0109 08DE            OLDCOD
```

allow the device to do the conversion from parallel data to serial data. One of the earliest large-scale-integration devices was the UART (Universal Asynchronous Receiver-Transmitter). It is still widely used and is made by several manufacturers. It is a 40-pin chip, and most often it requires 2 power supplies ($+5$ and -12 volts).

We have elected to use a more modern version of that chip, the Motorola MC6850 ACIA (Asynchronous Communications Interface Adapter), since it comes in a 24-pin package, requires only a single $+5$ volt supply, and can be set to a variety of modes under software control. This chip can be set up for our operation by the following POKEs:

10 POKE CONTROLREG, 19
20 POKE CONTROLREG, 17

where CONTROLREG is decimal 10240, the address to which the 6850 is wired. The first POKE resets the 6850, while the second POKE sets the chip for our 8-bit character with 2 stop bits. We can also accomplish the same setup in machine language.

After the 6850 setup, characters can be output by first testing to see if the previous character has been completed, then POKEing the character into the 6850's data register, illustrated by the following skeletal routine:

```
110 LET X = PEEK (STATUS)
120 (test for completion of previous character and loop to 110
    until 6850 is ready)
160 POKE DATAREG, CHARACTER
```

where CHARACTER must be ASCII-encoded and DATAREG is decimal 10241.

The actual routine we will use is machine-language code in a special ROM. The 6850 connections are shown in Figure 9-1, and the 6850 register details are in Table 9-2. You will note that the chip-select of the 6850 is connected to 1 of the 2K strobes we developed in Chapter 3.

TABLE 9-2: 6850 Register Selection

PIN 9	PIN 11	PIN 13	FUNCTION SELECTED
CS2	Reg. Sel. RS	R/W	
0	0	0	Write to control register
0	0	1	Read status register
0	1	0	Write to transmit register
0	1	1	Read receiver register
1	X	X	Disabled
STATUS REGISTER BITS			
Bit 0			High means receive data ready
Bit 1			High means okay to transmit
CONTROL REGISTER BITS			
Bits 0 and 1			Internal divide ratio (see text)
Bits 2, 3, 4			Word characteristics (number of bits, parity, etc.)
Bits 5 and 6			Interrupt controls

Let's be user-friendly

One possible scenario for a printer system could be operation in BASIC with just the hardware described so far, plus an appropriate baud-rate generator and a level shifter selected for your system (which will be described later). As an experiment, you may wish to set up what we just described, although you will not find it too practical. But here is the essence of such a system:

1. Create a look-up table to convert the first 64 of Sinclair's characters to ASCII. This routine is most easily done as a line 1 REM statement, starting off with 64 dummy characters after the REM and changing to their proper values by POKEs.
2. Set up a subroutine to print a single character. This routine would convert a Sinclair character to ASCII, test the ACIA for "ready," and output the character to the ACIA by means of a POKE.
3. Set up a modification of the preceding subroutine to print a series of ASCII characters for the carriage-return–line-feed function. Your printer may require a delay of several character-times after a carriage return. The limitations of this system will probably encourage you to read further. These limitations are:
    a. You must have the look-up table and printing subroutines resident in your BASIC program whenever printing is desired.
    b. Your routine must break out each character to be printed, including carriage returns and line feeds.
    c. Without going through great labor, you cannot list the program to the printer.
    d. LPRINT, LLIST, and COPY are not supported.

The rest of the chapter describes a more "user-friendly" printing system, which supports the preceding BASIC printing commands and requires no BASIC text overhead.

A ROM-based printer

The 8K Sinclair ROM supports only the Sinclair printer. If there were some way to substitute our own printer driver for Sinclair's, we could use most of the built-in BASIC printer functions with a serial printer of our own selection. This procedure is exactly our strategy.

All of Sinclair's character-printing functions are located at about $0800 and the 200 or so bytes following. Each time a character is to be printed, a flag is tested to determine whether the character goes to the video screen or to the printer. If the latter, a subroutine at $0851 is called to print 1 character. This subroutine, as well as the COPY routine, occupies

LISTING 9-2
Hex Dump of Printer ROM

```
*0800.08FF

0800-  18 03 CD 51 08 E1 D9 C9
0808-  57 ED 4B 39 40 79 FE 21
0810-  28 1A 3E 76 BA 28 30 2A
0818-  0E 40 BE 7A 20 20 0D 20
0820-  19 23 22 0E 40 0E 21 05
0828-  ED 43 39 40 78 FD BE 22
0830-  28 03 A7 20 DD 2E 04 C3
0838-  58 00 CD 9B 09 EB 77 23
0840-  22 0E 40 FD 35 39 C9 0E
0848-  21 05 FD CB 01 C6 C3 18
0850-  09 F5 3A 7B 40 A7 20 0D
0858-  3E 13 32 7B 40 32 00 28
0860-  3E 11 32 00 28 F1 18 25
0868-  00 16 16 2A 0C 40 23 18
0870-  43 06 05 3E 0D CD 80 08
0878-  10 F9 3E 0A 18 02 3E 20
0880-  F5 3A 00 28 E6 02 28 F9
0888-  F1 32 01 28 C9 FE 76 28
0890-  E0 A7 28 EA FE 40 30 E6
0898-  FE 26 38 04 C6 1B 18 E0
08A0-  FE 1C 38 04 C6 14 18 D8
08A8-  FE 0B 38 D2 21 C2 08 85
08B0-  6F 7E 18 CC 7E E5 CD 51
08B8-  08 E1 FE 0A 20 B0 15 20
08C0-  AD C9 00 00 00 00 00 00
08C8-  00 00 00 00 00 22 23 24
08D0-  3A 3F 28 29 3E 3C 3D 2B
08D8-  2D 2A 2F 3B 2C 2E CD 07
08E0-  02 C1 21 5C 40 36 76 06
08E8-  20 2B 36 00 10 FB 7D CB
08F0-  FF 32 38 40 C9 3E 17 90
08F8-  38 0B FD BE 22 DA 35 08
```

$0851–$08DD. Our revised printer routine is shown in Listing 9-1 in assembly-language format. We have preserved the following entry points:

$0851 Print a character
$0869 Copy the video screen
$0871 Do a carriage return/line feed

You will need to have a ROM of at least 256 bytes programmed with this code at relative addresses $0051 to $00DD, and the ROM contains original code at relative addresses $0000–$0050 and $00DE–$00FF. A hex dump of the entire 256 bytes is given in Listing 9-2. Perhaps a friend with a ROM programmer can program a 5-volt 2716 for you. Use a 350-nanosecond version or faster. This ROM is available for under $10. A programmed ROM can also be purchased by mail order* at a price of $30 postpaid. A listing of suitable 2716 ROMs is given in Table 9-3. If you use

*The Bit Stop, 5958 South Shenandoah Road, Mobile, Alabama 36608

TABLE 9-3: 2716 ROMs

EQUIVALENT 5-VOLT-ONLY 2Kx8 EPROMs	
Manufacturer	Part Number
AMD	Am 2716
Fairchild	2716
Fujitsu	MBM 2716
Hitachi	HM462716
Intel	2716
Mostek	MK2716
Motorola	MCM2716
NEC	MPD2716
Signetics	2716
Texas Instruments	TMS2516 (not TMS2716)

NOTE: TMS2716 (TI, Motorola) requires 3 power supplies and will *not* work.

a 2716 ROM, the unused portion (1–3/4K bytes) can be used for other programs, such as the dumb-terminal routine presented in Chapter 10.

The schematic of our circuit in Figure 8-1 shows how a 2716 is wired into the system. You will need to modify the ROM decoder circuit on the expansion board as shown in Figure 9-3 for the printer ROM. The revised circuit activates the new ROM at $08XX addresses and simultaneously deactivates the Sinclair ROM, so that any printer instructions are derived from the new patch ROM.

For the Z80 machine-language buff, the new routine sets up the ACIA before the first character is printed and sets a flag to signal initialization. If the character is RETURN, a line feed and 5 carriage returns are printed—5 because many printers require the extra time! Alphabetical and numeric characters are converted to ASCII by adding constants, while punctuation characters are converted by table lookup. Graphics and inverted characters are converted to space. COPY gets every character from the display file and prints until all 24 lines are processed. Finally the printing program is split up because of the necessity for preserving original Sinclair entry-points.

Note that if you have a fancy printer, you must select (by switches or jumpers) its nonautomatic line-feed option, since we output our own line feeds. If you find that you get 6 spaces between lines, then you probably need to adjust your printer. Consult your printer operating manual.

In order to employ this user-friendly system, it will be necessary to make minor changes to some BASIC programs, since line-formatting statements such as the tab- and print-field spacing with the comma are not supported.

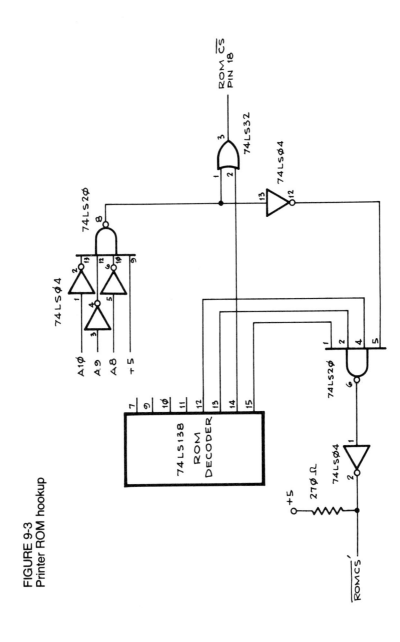

FIGURE 9-3
Printer ROM hookup

ACIA addresses

In Figure 9-1 we show the ACIA register select (RS) pin connected to the expansion bus address line A0. From Table 9-2 you will see that the CONTROL or STATUS registers will be selected when RS is low and the DATA registers selected when RS is high. This situation means that the CONTROL or STATUS register is selected by an *even* address and the DATA registers by an *odd* address. Whether we are writing to the CONTROL register or reading the STATUS register is determined by the R/W pin hooked to WR. The 6850 chip select is tied to the line in our ROM decoder that reflects addresses $2800–$2FFF. As a practical matter, any even address in this range selects CONTROL or STATUS, and any odd address selects DATA. For uniformity, we have used $2800 (decimal 10240) as the even address and $2801 (decimal 10241) as the odd address.

Okay, so we have used 2K of address space where only 2 bytes are required. But remember that Sinclair used 32K for 1K or 2K of RAM! Actually, if you need the address space, you can buy the extra chips to decode further.

Level shifting

The 6850 ACIA outputs serial characters over its TXD line, Pin 6. The idle condition is at the TTL high level (3–4 volts). Most commercial printers cannot operate directly from the TTL level signal. The type of level shifting to use depends on your printer's requirements. Refer to Chapter 11 for details of level-shifting circuits.

Baud-rate generators

ACIAs and UARTs require a clock that runs at a multiple of the baud rate. In our case, we need a clock that runs at a frequency 16 times the desired baud rate. For example, if the printer operates at 110 baud, the ACIA clock should run at 16×110 or 1760 hertz. We offer 3 models of baud-rate generators in increasing order of cost in the following discussions.

The Stick-Shift Baud-Rate Generator

A simple LM555 circuit, shown in Figure 9-4, provides a pot-adjustable frequency source that can be used as the ACIA clock. There are 2 methods of tuning to correct frequency:

FIGURE 9-4
Baud-rate generator using 555. A very simple
adjustable frequency source.

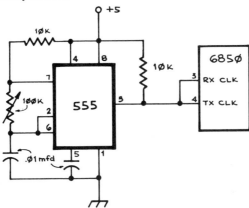

1. Use a friend's frequency counter. Set the output to 16 times the desired baud rate.

2. Print a repetitive pattern from a BASIC program and adjust the potentiometer until the printout is correct. Then move slightly in both directions until misprinting occurs and try to leave the pot halfway between those 2 extremes. A pattern of alternating Us and *s gives the bits a lot of exercise.

The Overdrive Baud-Rate Generator

A higher-cost alternative is shown in Figure 9-5. It derives its basic frequency from the Sinclair's clock, which runs at 3.25 MHz. Dividing by 21 occurs in the pair of 74LS193s and results in a frequency near 153,600 Hz, the frequency required for 9600 baud. Repeated division by 2 in the 4024 chip results in 4800, 2400, 1200, 600, 300, 150, and 75 baud signals (note that 110 baud is missing from this list). Simply wire your selected signal to 6850 Pins 3 and 4.

Since the Sinclair's clock is crystal controlled, all these baud rates will be exact, with no adjustment required. If you wish to change baud rates without rewiring, an 8-position DIP switch can be used on your board.

The Automatic-Transmission Baud-Rate Generator

For about 15 bucks you can generate baud-rate signals with a chip designed specifically for the purpose. It requires its own crystal for frequency control. See Figure 9-6 for the schematic of the MC14411.

FIGURE 9-5
Baud-rate generator using counters. Most of the
standard baud rates are available. They are derived
from the Sinclair's clock.

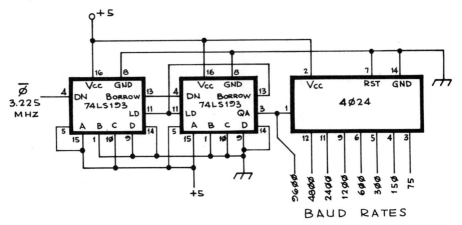

Debugging your circuit

Erratic operation of the printer is usually related to misadjustment of the baud rate. If 1 of the data lines to the 6850 is not connected properly, half the characters will print as duplicates of other characters.

If no printing occurs, touch a voltmeter or logic probe to the TXD (Pin 6) line of the 6850 while attempting to print. If pulses appear, the problem is downstream from 6850. If no pulses occur, check your wiring, including the baud-rate clock.

A dead Sinclair generally signals a wiring error, probably in the ROM circuitry. A slow ROM can also be the cause. Horizontal bars on your TV indicate power-supply overload.

Interfacing to parallel printers

The serial-printer software described on page 109 can be used without change to operate a parallel printer provided that different interface hardware is used. The hardware, while simple, is necessarily much changed to accommodate a parallel printer.

About parallel printers

Most parallel printers currently available are identical in the connections required to interface to their host computer. New parallel printers start at prices near the $300 level and go up in price to well into 4 figures. Almost

118

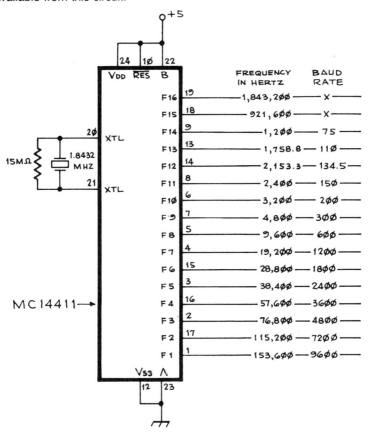

FIGURE 9-6
Baud-rate generator using MC14411. All standard rates
are available from this circuit.

all operate with the ASCII character set but differ greatly in speed of operation, special control features such as automatic form-feed, ability to print graphics, width of paper, and so on. The list of parallel ASCII printer makers includes Epson, Centronics, Radio Shack, C. Itoh, and many others. Our tests were run on an Epson MX70 originally hooked to an Apple computer; the original cable was simply brought to the Sinclair expansion board.

Parallel printers are line oriented; they generally will print nothing until a carriage-return character is sent. The printer accepts the printable characters very rapidly and accumulates them in a buffer until the entire line is ready to print; it starts the printing operation when the carriage-return signal arrives or when the printer's buffer is full. The designation *parallel* refers to the 7 or 8 parallel wires over which the characters are transmitted.

119

Transmission of character data can be very fast over 8 wires, in contrast to the speed of serial-data transfer.

These printers have at least 2 control signals, $\overline{\text{STR}}$ and $\overline{\text{ACK}}$; the STROBE signal is generated by the interface to tell the printer that a valid character is on the 8 data wires. The ACKNOWLEDGE signal is generated by the printer to tell the interface that the preceding character has been processed. Data and control signals are at the TTL level (0–5 volts) and can come directly from standard TTL logic chips. The $\overline{\text{ACK}}$ signal from the printer will be delayed upon transmission of the carriage return, since at this point the printer is busy printing the entire line.

While the standard parallel-printer connector has 36 positions, we will use only 20 wires, with the signals over wires 1–10 and ground returns over wires 19–28. These 20 positions are in a physical cluster so that a standard 20-wire ribbon cable can be used. Press-on insulation-displacement connectors are preferred to solder-type connectors. An Apple dealer may have such a cable already made up. The interface end of the cable is a 20-position socket (2 rows of 10 holes) that can be plugged into a matching pin connector glued to your expansion board to which you can solder the 20 required wires. Double check to be sure that your connections are correct and in accordance with your printer specifications.

The interface hardware

About 7 integrated circuits are used in the interface; we are purposefully vague about the exact number because if you already have, for example, unused OR gates available on the board, there is no need to add another 74LS32; similarly, check your availability of inverter gates before adding another 74LS04.

The interface schematic is shown in Figure 9-7. One of the strobes ($2800) from the ROM decoder is used to activate the interface. It is gated with A0, so that even addresses read the "status" of the interface and odd addresses latch the data into the 74LS175s. This latter signal triggers the 74LS123 one-shot to provide the $\overline{\text{STR}}$ signal to the printer after a character is latched. This signal also resets the ACK flip-flop (two 74LS10 gates cross-coupled) to be able to signal "busy" to the computer via the 74LS125 gate. The flip-flop is not set again until the printer provides its $\overline{\text{ACK}}$ signal, a low-going pulse (the Sinclair $\overline{\text{RST}}$ signal does place the flip-flop in a known state upon power-up, signaling "not busy").

We bring the STATUS signal back to the Sinclair via data line D1 in order to make the interface software the same for both the serial and the parallel printers. Forethought is the lazy man's tool.

FIGURE 9-7
Parallel printer interface schematic. Circuit generates
printer STROBE and receives printer ACK.

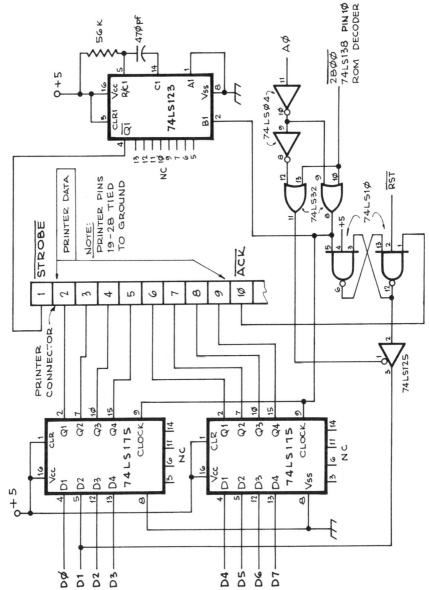

Operation will be the most convenient if you use the printer ROM described on page 113, although you can theoretically print using PEEKs to determine interface status and POKEs to print characters. The ROM circuit is identical to that for the serial printer.

Debugging

If you have any difficulty, first remember that your printer probably requires a carriage-return character before its mechanical whirs and clicks will start, even though you have sent the characters of HELLO JOE to its buffer. If the Sinclair appears dead, it is probably waiting for the status to be high, so check 74LS10 Pin 12. If Pin 12 is low, turn the printer off, then on, to convince the printer to provide its startup $\overline{ACK}$.

Another check is to make sure a short low-going pulse appears on the 74LS123 Pin 4 each time a character is POKEd into address $2801. A logic probe is necessary to detect this pulse of only 10 microseconds.

The Sinclair may ''hang-up'' (appear inactive or dead) if the printer is not powered-up or if the cable is not connected at both ends.

If all is well, you may LPRINT within your program, LLIST the programs, and COPY the screen to the printer. See the comments on serial printers on page 114 if your printed lines are widely spaced; you may need to change a switch or jumper in your printer to defeat its auto-line-feed.

Damage to the interface and/or printer can occur if your cable connections are incorrect. Be sure to check and recheck your wiring before applying power to the computer and printer. Be sure power and ground connections are applied to all ICs. Here is a checklist:

1. The 10 ground wires should be connected to pins that your printer manual calls ''ground'' or ''signal return.''
2. The 74LS123 output Pin 4 should go to the pin your printer manual calls ''$\overline{STR}$'' or ''$\overline{STROBE}$.''
3. The 74LS10 input Pin 1 should be connected to the printer's $\overline{ACK}$ pin.
4. The printer manual may call the data lines D1 through D8. If so, they should be derived from Sinclair's lines D0 through D7 respectively. If the printer uses only 7 data lines, use Sinclair's lines D0 through D6.

10

THE SINCLAIR
AS A DUMB TERMINAL

Talk to the big campus computer from a Sinclair at your house? Or tie into the company's computer network? Are we dreaming?

No, with a relatively minor expansion plus the purchase of a telephone interface (called a *modem*), these things are possible. We'll show you the details of the expansion and give some general information about how the phone connections are made, so you will be in a position to use your Sinclair for this purpose.

Normally a terminal is used for accessing the big central computer over the phone system. It can be a *dumb* device, meaning it simply prints or places incoming characters on a CRT and sends characters from a keyboard to the central computer. The terminal may be simply a Teletype®, or it can be a smarter device whose cost can run into thousands. For example, a smart terminal might allow storage of incoming data on disk systems.

Modems

The most common rate of data transmission over ordinary phone lines is either 110 baud or 300 baud (see page 105 for the meaning of baud rate), and the character code is almost always ASCII. The 300 baud transmission rate is the maximum that can be achieved reliably with ordinary inexpensive equipment.

123

The purpose of a *modem* (modulator-demodulator) between the terminal and the phone lines is to generate and receive audio tones in the range suitable for phone transmission and to assure that neither the terminal nor the phone system is harmed by the connection. The modem may be a physical wire connection or an acoustic connection; the latter uses a cradle into which you place the telephone handset. The telephone company takes a dim view of amateurs connecting into their equipment, and we therefore recommend purchase of a commercial modem approved for use. Follow the procedures recommended by the modem manufacturer for notifying the telephone company. The problems of designing and building a modem are quite formidable, since the device must generate a transmit tone (relatively loud) and receive a different tone from miles away (relatively weak) over the same pair of wires and filter one tone from the other. You will note that in this system, characters are traveling in both directions at the same time. The terminal must not lose incoming characters while it is sending characters from its keyboard.

Full versus half duplex

There are certain characteristics of each big system that must be paralleled by your system. For example, the big guy may require 2 stop bits in his character format. Also there are always protocol requirements, such as typing a password to access the system. You must know whether you want to talk BASIC, FORTRAN, COBOL, or whatever the system supports, and so on. The central computer may operate in full-duplex, half-duplex, or either (your choice). In full-duplex, your terminal does not put your key presses on your screen; rather the central computer "echoes" your characters. Full-duplex is generally preferred. In the half-duplex mode, your computer must display the characters you enter on the keyboard.

A block diagram of the connections required for a Sinclair dumb-terminal system is shown in Figure 10-1. The expansion board is required, and it should contain the 6850 ACIA described on page 111. It simultaneously converts the Sinclair parallel data to serial for outgoing characters and the serial data to parallel for incoming characters. The modem should be RS232, and consequently you will require level shifting to and from TTL levels, as described in Chapter 11. The dumb modems are the most adaptable, and they are advertised in the $100–$150 range. Forget auto-dial, auto-answer, and so on.

Perhaps you wish to experiment before you enter the "big time." Figure 10-1 also shows how you can hook up 2 expanded Sinclair computers to talk to each other in the same room over a few feet of wire; level

FIGURE 10-1
Connections for the dumb terminal. *Top*: connecting to
phone lines. *Bottom*: hooking 2 Sinclairs together.

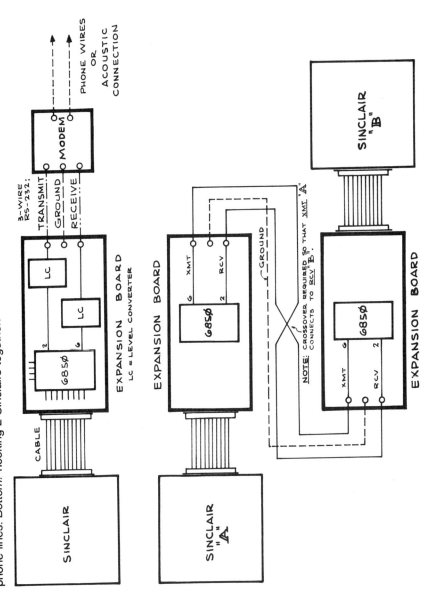

conversion is not required in this case, although if you wish to communicate the length of the house, level conversion may be required on both computers. Do *not* feed a higher-voltage RS232 signal into a TTL device without level conversion. You will not like the results.

Requirements on the expansion board

At this point, we can simply tell you which of the building blocks from previous chapters you will need, and you can assemble them into your dumb-terminal system. You will need the 6850 ACIA and ROM decoder modifications given on pages 106–111. Since the 6850 will be used in both directions, we will also use the receive-data pin. We will locate the 6850 at the same address as the printer (the $2800 group of addresses). The most difficult addition is software to run your unit as a dumb terminal, and we recommend that it be placed in ROM. It may be placed in the same 2716 ROM as that containing the printer software. 1 additional wire, shown in Figure 10-2, must be added to the ROM decoder circuit of Figure 9-3 to access the program at addresses $2100 and following. If you do not care to program your own ROM, you may buy one for $30 from The Bit Stop, 5958 South Shenandoah Road, Mobile, Alabama 36608.

You will need 1 of the baud-rate generators set to 16 times your selected baud rate, probably 16 × 300 or 4800 Hz. You will also need level shifting for both directions.

The software

Design of the software is more than the beginning programmer can expect to accomplish; so we have included a tested program in Listing 10-1. The software must be fast enough to avoid missing characters, so machine

FIGURE 10-2
Modification to the ROM decoder in Figure 9-3 to enable
the dumb terminal ROM at $3400–$34FF

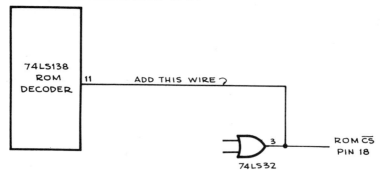

LISTING 10-1
Dumb Terminal Software

```
                        TITLE     'ZX81 TERMINAL PROGRAM'
                        ;
                        ;    JULY 13, 1982
                        ;    BY DON RINDSBERG
                        ;
0000'                        ASEG
                             .Z80

                        ;
                        ; SCRATCH PAD:
                        ;
403F                    HDX       EQU    403FH    ;ZERO = FULL DPLX
                                                  ;NONZERO = HALF DPLX
4040                    KEYREL    EQU    4040H    ;ZERO = KEY RELEASED
4041                    PRTCNT    EQU    4041H    ;VIDEO CHARACTER COUNTER
4042                    BUFCNT    EQU    4042H    ;# OF CHARS IN BUFFER
4043                    INPTR     EQU    4043H    ;BUFFER INPUT POINTER
4045                    OUTPTR    EQU    4045H    ;BUFFER OUTPUT POINTER
4047                    BUFFER    EQU    4047H    ;KEY BUFFER

                        ;
                        ; ROM ROUTINES:
                        ;
02BB                    KBD       EQU    2BBH     ;PUTS KEY CODE IN H,L
07BD                    KBDEC     EQU    7BDH     ;KEYPRESS DECODE IN B,C
0C0E                    SCROLL    EQU    0C0EH    ;SCROLLS VIDEO SCREEN

                        ;
                        ; HARDWARE ADDRESSES:
                        ;
2800                    STATUS    EQU    2800H    ;ACIA STATUS REGISTER
2800                    CONTRL    EQU    2800H    ;ACIA CONTROL REGISTER
2801                    DATARG    EQU    2801H    ;ACIA DATA REGISTER
                                                  ; (REC AND XMIT)

                        ;
2100                    ORIGIN    EQU    2100H    ;START OF THIS PROGRAM
                        ;
                                  ORG    ORIGIN   ;BEGIN HERE
2100    06 17           SETUP:    LD     B,17H    ;GET SCRATCH COUNT
2102    21 4040                   LD     HL,4040H ;BEGIN SCRATCH
2105    AF                        XOR    A        ;CLEAR A
2106    77              ZERO:     LD     (HL),A   ;CLEAR A BYTE
2107    23                        INC    HL       ;BUMP POINTER
2108    10 FC                     DJNZ   ZERO     ;LOOP UNTIL DONE
210A    2F                        CPL             ;GET NONZERO
210B    32 4040                   LD     (KEYREL),A ;TRICK KEY RELEASE
210E    21 4047                   LD     HL,BUFFER  ;SET UP BUFFER
2111    22 4043                   LD     (INPTR),HL ;INPUT POINTER
2114    22 4045                   LD     (OUTPTR),HL ;OUTPUT POINTER
2117    3E 13                     LD     A,13H    ;RESET BYTE
2119    32 2800                   LD     (CONTRL),A ;TO ACIA
211C    3E 11                     LD     A,11H    ;CHARACTER FORMAT
211E    32 2800                   LD     (CONTRL),A ;TO ACIA
2121    CD 0C0E                   CALL   SCROLL   ;START VID AT BOTTOM
2124    3A 2800         INCHR:    LD     A,(STATUS) ;ACIA STATUS
2127    E6 01                     AND    1        ;RECEIVE CHARACTER?
2129    28 42                     JR     Z,KEYPR  ;JUMP IF NOT
212B    3A 2801                   LD     A,(DATARG) ;GET INPUT CHAR
212E    E6 7F                     AND    7FH      ;MASK BIT 7
2130    FE 0D                     CP     0DH      ;CARRIAGE RET?
2132    20 09                     JR     NZ,CONVRT ;JUMP IF NOT
2134    CD 0C0E                   CALL   SCROLL   ;DO THE <CR>
2137    AF                        XOR    A        ;CLEAR A
2138    32 4041                   LD     (PRTCNT),A ;ZERO CHAR COUNT
213B    18 30                     JR     KEYPR    ;GET KEYPRESS
213D    FE 5B           CONVRT:   CP     5BH      ;GREATER THAN Z?
213F    30 2C                     JR     NC,KEYPR ;IF SO, IGNORE
2141    FE 41                     CP     41H      ;LESS THAN A?
2143    38 04                     JR     C,CONV2  ;IF SO, TEST MORE
2145    D6 1B                     SUB    1BH      ;ASCII TO SINCLAIR
2147    18 0E                     JR     OUTCH    ;PRINT LETTER
2149    FE 20           CONV2:    CP     20H      ;LESS THAN SPACE?
```

127

```
214B    38 20              JR      C,KEYPR      ;IF SO, IGNORE
214D    21 2200            LD      HL,TABLE-20H ;GET TABLE
2150    85                 ADD     A,L          ;CALCULATE POSITION
2151    6F                 LD      L,A          ;TO H,L
2152    7E                 LD      A,(HL)       ;LOOK UP CHARACTER
2153    17                 RLA                  ;TEST FOR MINUS
2154    38 17              JR      C,KEYPR      ;IGNORE MINUSES
2156    1F                 RRA                  ;RESTORE CHARACTER
2157    D7         OUTCH:  RST     10H          ;TO VIDEO
2158    3A 4041            LD      A,(PRTCNT)   ;GET COLUMN
215B    3C                 INC     A            ;BUMP COUNT
215C    32 4041            LD      (PRTCNT),A   ;STORE COLUMN
215F    D6 20              SUB     20H          ;32 CHARS?
2161    20 0A              JR      NZ,KEYPR
2163    32 4041            LD      (PRTCNT),A   ;ZERO COUNT
2166    CD 0C0E            CALL    SCROLL       ;SCROLL SCREEN
2169    00                 NOP                  ;SPACE
216A    00                 NOP
216B    00                 NOP
216C    00                 NOP
216D    CD 02BB    KEYPR:  CALL    KBD          ;GET KEYBRD STATUS
2170    44                 LD      B,H          ;COPY
2171    4D                 LD      C,L          ; TO B,C
2172    2C                 INC     L            ;WAS L=0FFH?
2173    20 06              JR      NZ,YESKEY    ;IF NOT, KEY
2175    24                 INC     H            ;WAS H=0FFH?
2176    28 0B              JR      Z,NOKEY      ;IF SO, NO KEY
2178    24                 INC     H            ;WAS H=0FEH?
2179    28 08              JR      Z,NOKEY      ;IF SO, A SHIFT
217B    3A 4040    YESKEY: LD      A,(KEYREL)   ;GET FLAG
217E    A7                 AND     A            ;TEST
217F    28 35              JR      Z,NEWKEY     ;JUMP IF NEW KEY
2181    20 04              JR      NZ,CHKBUF    ;JUMP IF NOT
2183    AF         NOKEY:  XOR     A            ;CLEAR A
2184    32 4040            LD      (KEYREL),A   ;ZERO FLAG
2187    3A 4042    CHKBUF: LD      A,(BUFCNT)   ;ANY IN BUFFER?
218A    A7                 AND     A            ;TEST
218B    28 07              JR      Z,LINK       ;JUMP IF NONE
218D    3A 2800            LD      A,(STATUS)   ;ACIA BUSY?
2190    E6 02              AND     2            ;MASK XMIT BIT
2192    20 02              JR      NZ,OUTPUT    ;JUMP IF READY
2194    18 8E      LINK:   JR      INCHR        ;TO BEGINNING
2196    2A 4045    OUTPUT: LD      HL,(OUTPTR)  ;GET POINTER
2199    7E                 LD      A,(HL)       ;CHAR FROM BUFFER
219A    23                 INC     HL           ;BUMP POINTER
219B    F5                 PUSH    AF           ;SAVE CHARACTER
219C    7D                 LD      A,L          ;TEST FOR END
219D    FE 57              CP      57H          ;  OF BUFFER
219F    20 02              JR      NZ,STORE     ;JUMP IF NOT END
21A1    2E 47              LD      L,47H        ;GET BUFFER START
21A3    22 4045    STORE:  LD      (OUTPTR),HL  ;SAVE POINTER
21A6    F1                 POP     AF           ;GET CHARACTER
21A7    32 2801            LD      (DATARG),A   ;  TO ACIA
21AA    00                 NOP
21AB    00                 NOP
21AC    00                 NOP
21AD    3A 4042            LD      A,(BUFCNT)   ;DECREMENT BUFFER
21B0    3D                 DEC     A            ;  COUNTER
21B1    32 4042            LD      (BUFCNT),A   ;SAVE NEW COUNT
21B4    18 DE      LINK2:  JR      LINK         ;TO BEG VIA LINK
21B6    3A 4042    NEWKEY: LD      A,(BUFCNT)   ;GET CHAR COUNT
21B9    D6 10              SUB     10H          ;TOO MANY?
21BB    28 F7              JR      Z,LINK2      ;BACK TO BEGINNING
21BD    32 4040    SETKRL: LD      (KEYREL),A   ;NONZERO TO KEYREL
21C0    CD 07BD            CALL    KBDEC        ;DECODE THE KEY
21C3    3A 403F            LD      A,(HDX)      ;FULL DUPLEX?
21C6    A7                 AND     A
21C7    28 27              JR      Z,CONVERT    ;SKIP IF FULL DPLX
21C9    7E         TOVID:  LD      A,(HL)       ;GET CHARACTER
21CA    FE 76              CP      76H          ;IS IT ENTER?
21CC    28 19              JR      Z,SCRLL      ;SCROLL IF ENTER
```

128

```
21CE   FE 40              CP      40H           ;GREATER THAN Z?
21D0   30 1E              JR      NC,CONVERT    ;IGNORE
21D2   A7                 AND     A             ;TEST FOR SPACE
21D3   28 04              JR      Z,OUT         ;OUTPUT IF SPACE
21D5   FE 0B              CP      0BH           ;LESS THAN PUNCT
21D7   38 17              JR      C, CONVERT    ;IGNORE
21D9   E5          OUT:   PUSH    HL            ;SAVE TABLE POINTER
21DA   D7                 RST     10H           ;TO VIDEO
21DB   E1                 POP     HL            ;RESTORE POINTER
21DC   3A 4041            LD      A,(PRTCNT)    ;NEED TO SCROLL?
21DF   3C                 INC     A             ;INC CHAR COUNT
21E0   32 4041            LD      (PRTCNT),A    ;SAVE NEW COUNT
21E3   D6 20              SUB     20H           ;32 CHARS?
21E5   20 09              JR      NZ,CONVERT    ;JUMP IF NOT
21E7   E5          SCRLL: PUSH    HL            ;SAVE TABLE POINTER
21E8   CD 0C0E            CALL    SCROLL        ;SCROLL SCREEN
21EB   E1                 POP     HL            ;RESTORE POINTER
21EC   AF                 XOR     A             ;CLEAR A
21ED   32 4041            LD      (PRTCNT),A    ;ZERO COUNTER
21F0   01 21C3     CONVERT:LD     BC,QWERTY-7EH ;TABLE BASE
21F3   09                 ADD     HL,BC         ;CALC TABLE POSIT
21F4   7E                 LD      A,(HL)        ;GET ASCI CHAR
21F5   FE 05              CP      5             ;CONTROL E?
                                                ;(CHANGE IF DESIRED)
21F7   20 02              JR      NZ,TOBUFF     ;JUMP IF NOT
21F9   CF                 RST     8             ;TO BASIC VIA ERROR
21FA   10                 DB      10H           ;ERROR H
21FB   2A 4043     TOBUFF:LD      HL,(INPTR)    ;GET BUFFER POINTER
21FE   77                 LD      (HL),A        ;CHAR TO BUFFER
21FF   23                 INC     HL            ;BUMP POINTER
2200   7D                 LD      A,L           ;LOW BYTE TO A
2201   FE 57              CP      57H           ;END OF BUFFER?
2203   20 02              JR      NZ,STOR       ;JUMP IF NOT
2205   2E 47              LD      L,47H         ;WRAPAROUND
2207   22 4043     STOR:  LD      (INPTR),HL    ;SAVE POINTER
220A   3A 4042            LD      A,(BUFCNT)    ;GET CHAR COUNT
220D   3C                 INC     A             ;BUMP COUNT
220E   32 4042            LD      (BUFCNT),A    ;SAVE NEW COUNT
2211   18 81              JR      LINK          ;TO BEGINNING
                   ;
2213                      DS      13            ;HACKER SPACE
                   ;
2220   00 FF 0B 0C  TABLE: DB     0,0FFH,0BH,0CH,0DH,0FFH,0FFH
2224   0D FF FF
2227   FF 10 11 17         DB     0FFH,10H,11H,17H,15H,1AH,16H
222B   15 1A 16
222E   1B 18 1C 1D         DB     1BH,18H,1CH,1DH,1EH,1FH,20H
2232   1E 1F 20
2235   21 22 23 24         DB     21H,22H,23H,24H,25H,0EH,19H
2239   25 0E 19
223C   12 14 13 0F         DB     12H,14H,13H,0FH,0FFH
2240   FF

                   ;
                   ; 0FFH = NOT USED  (IN TABLE ABOVE)
                   ;
2241   5A 58 43 56  QWERTY: DB    'ZXCVASDFGQWERT12'
2245   41 53 44 46
2249   47 51 57 45
224D   52 54 31 32
2251   33 34 35 30         DB     '34509876POIUY',0DH,'LK'
2255   39 38 37 36
2259   50 4F 49 55
225D   59 0D 4C 4B
2261   4A 48 20 2E         DB     'JH .MNB:;?/',1,13H,4,6,7
2265   4D 4E 42 3A
2269   3B 3F 2F 01
226D   13 04 06 07
2271   11 17 05 12         DB     11H,17H,5,12H,14H,1BH,2,18H
2275   14 1B 02 18
2279   03 08 7F 0C         DB     3,8,7FH,0CH,9,1AH,0AH,'"'
227D   09 1A 0A 22
```

```
2281    29 28 24 19        DB      ')($',19H,0DH,'=+-^#,)(*'
2285    0D 3D 2B 2D
2289    5E 23 2C 3E
228D    3C 2A
                    ;
                    ;
                    END     ORIGIN
```

language must be used rather than BASIC. It must never get tied up—for example, in an output loop—or incoming characters will be missed. The software is as busy as a one-man band who never stops; when the score calls for a drum beat, he beats the drum regardless of the harmonica score. The software keeps looping, checking for incoming characters, checking for key presses, and checking for outgoing characters. In order to avoid a short loop, key presses are placed into a 16-character buffer immediately, avoiding a situation whereby the program must wait for the ACIA to be ready to transmit.

In order to be compatible with other systems, the Sinclair-coded keys must be converted to ASCII for transmission. This conversion is accomplished by lookup in the table called QWERTY, which is a parallel to the lookup table at $007E in the 8K ROM. Likewise incoming ASCII characters must be converted to Sinclair code. This conversion is done for letters and numbers by simply subtracting constants; it is done for punctuation characters by lookup in TABLE, which contains the Sinclair code for punctuation, with $FF in the positions that represent ASCII characters not supported by Sinclair.

Control codes

Big central computers usually require some of the ASCII control codes for access. We have included the more popular control codes in QWERTY in order to transmit a control code when certain shifted keys are pressed, since we have no use for the keywords and functions. Details are given in Table 10-1. A shifted E is used to return you to BASIC. If you require different control codes from those in Table 10-1, you can make a substitution in the ROM. For example, if you need control-K and do not need control-Z, find the $1A in the table and substitute $0B. This method works for any change except the control-E return to BASIC; if you wish to change that, change the byte at $21F6, which now contains $05 or control-E (E stands for exit).

Starting up

You must first decide whether to operate in half- or full-duplex. If you are in doubt, start off in half-duplex, and if the big guy is operating in

TABLE 10-1: Control Keys Available

FUNCTION	KEY	HEX	ASCII MNEMONIC
Control A	Shift A	01	SOH
Control B	Shift 2	02	STX
Control C	Shift 4	03	ETX
Control D	Shift D	04	EOT
Control E*	Shift E*	05*	ENQ*
Control F	Shift F	06	ACK
Control G	Shift G	07	BEL
Control H	Shift 5	08	BS
Control I	Shift 8	09	HT
Control J	Shift 6	OA	LF
Control L	Shift 9	OC	FF
Control M	ENTER	OD	CR
Control Q	Shift Q	11	DC1
Control R	Shift R	12	DC2
Control S	Shift S	13	DC3
Control T	Shift T	14	DC4
Control W	Shift W	17	ETB
Control X	Shift 3	18	CAN
Control Y	Shift Y	19	EM
Control Z	Shift 7	1A	SUB
Control [	Shift 1	1B	ESC
DELETE	Shift 0	7F	DEL
Up Arrow	Shift H	5E	∧

NOTE: Control K, N, O, P, U, V not available. See page 130 if any of these is required.

*Control E is programmed to return to BASIC.

full-duplex, you will get double characters on your screen. To set the half-duplex flag, POKE address 16447 with a number not 0.

The dumb-terminal machine language can then be entered by a USR call. The entire start-up program to RUN is:

```
10 POKE 16447,1 (use 0 for full-duplex)
20 RAND USR 8448
```

To return to BASIC, press shifted-E. If you need to shift to full-duplex

```
POKE 16447,0
```

Default is full-duplex.

Warning: The assembler that generated the code in Listing 10-1 places 2-byte addresses such that they are readable as addresses. If you are entering hexadecimal code, *reverse* the 2 address bytes. Better still, enter from the hex dump in Listing 10-2.

```
0100  06172140  40AF7723  10FC2F32  40402147  ..!ƏƏ.wₙ../2ƏƏ!G
0110  40224340  2245403E  13320028  3E113200  Ə"CƏ"EƏ>.2.<>.2.
0120  28CD0E0C  3A0028E6  0128423A  0128E67F  (..:.(..(B:.(..
0130  FE0D2009  CD0E0CAF  32414018  30FE5B30  .. .....2AƏ.0.[0
0140  2CFE4138  04D61B18  0EFE2038  20210022  .. .... 8 !."
0150  856F7E17  38171FD7  3A41403C  324140D6  .o~.8...:AƏ<2AƏ.
0160  20200A32  4140CD0E  0C000000  00CDBB02  .2AƏ.........
0170  444D2C20  0624280B  2428083A  4040A728  DM, .$<.$<.:ƏƏ.(
0180  352004AF  3240403A  4240A728  073A0028  5 ..2ƏƏ:BƏ.(.:.(
0190  E6022002  188E2A45  407E23F5  7DFE5720  .. ...*EƏ~ₙ.).W
01A0  022E4722  4540F132  01280000  003A4240  ..G"EƏ.2.<...:BƏ
01B0  3D324240  18DE3A42  40D61028  F7324040  =2BƏ..:BƏ..(.2ƏƏ
01C0  CDBD073A  3F40A728  277EFE76  2819FE40  ...:?Ə.('~.ᴠ(..Ə
01D0  301EA728  04FE0B38  17E5D7E1  3A41403C  0..(..8....:AƏ<
01E0  324140D6  202009E5  CD0E0CE1  AF324140  2AƏ. ......2AƏ
01F0  01C32109  7EFE0520  02CF102A  43407723  ..!.~.. ...*CƏwₙ
0200  7DFE5720  022E4722  43403A42  403C3242  ).W ..G"CƏ:BƏ<2B
0210  40188100  00000000  00000000  00000000  Ə............
0220  00FF0B0C  0DFFFFFF  10111715  1A161B18  ...............
0230  1C1D1E1F  20212223  24250E19  1214130F  .... !"#$%......
0240  FF5A5843  56415344  46475157  45525431  .ZXCᴠASDFGQWERT1
0250  32333435  30393837  36504F49  55590D4C  234509876POIUY.L
0260  4B4A4820  2E4D4E42  3A3B3F2F  01130406  KJH .MNB:;?/....
0270  07111705  12141B02  1803087F  0C091A0A  ...............
0280  22292824  190D3D2B  2D5E232C  3E3C2AFF  ")($..=+-^#,><*.
0290  FFFFFFFF  FFFFFFFF  FFFFFFFF  FFFFFFFF  ...............
02A0  FFFFFFFF  FFFFFFFF  FFFFFFFF  FFFFFFFF  ...............
02B0  FFFFFFFF  FFFFFFFF  FFFFFFFF  FFFFFFFF  ...............
02C0  FFFFFFFF  FFFFFFFF  FFFFFFFF  FFFFFFFF  ...............
02D0  FFFFFFFF  FFFFFFFF  FFFFFFFF  FFFFFFFF  ...............
02E0  FFFFFFFF  FFFFFFFF  FFFFFFFF  FFFFFFFF  ...............
02F0  FFFFFFFF  FFFFFFFF  FFFFFFFF  FFFFFFFF  ...............
```

Software modifications

If you want the ACIA to be at another pair of addresses, move to another pin in the decoder and change the instructions at $2119, $211E, $2124, $212B, $218B, and $21A7.

If you wish to relocate the entire program to a different address, the only addresses that require change are those referring to the tables, since the remainder of the program uses relative addresses. The instructions at $214D and $21FO must be changed. Note that the addresses in the program are offset by constants from the actual table addresses.

For a better understanding of the software, Sinclair ROM routines are used by the dumb terminal software.

KBD	$02BB	Places key press in HL
KBDEC	$07BD	Decodes key press into a table address in HL
SCROLL	$OCOE	Scrolls the video screen
OUTCH	RST10	Outputs a character to video
ERROR	RST8	To BASIC via error routine

Temporary storage of pointers, key-press characters, and so on is in the Sinclair printer buffer. We use 24 bytes starting at $403F. This space is used only by the Sinclair-built printer.

The hex machine code is written to start at address $2100. When this code is placed in a 2716 ROM, it should start at relative address $0100; the printer routines (see pages 109–113) occupy the first $100 (256) bytes. The ROM wiring we have given on pages 114–115 generates an image of $0800–$08FF at $2000–$20FF, so the latter addresses cannot be used. But there is plenty of space for your further additions, i.e., it exists at $228F–$27FF and contains something over 1¼K out of the 2K ROM.

11

LEVEL-SHIFTING CIRCUITS FOR THE PRINTER AND THE DUMB TERMINAL

Having decided to build the printer or dumb-terminal interface, you next must determine what kind of signal your printer or host system requires. Unfortunately there are currently 4 different conventions in common usage that confuse the issue a little. Remember that each character to be transmitted is determined by an 8-bit code. These characters can be sent in 1 of 2 ways. The first is by 8 parallel lines, each carrying 1 bit of the code. This type of interface was described in detail on pages 118–122. The other way to send the 8 bits of the information is by serial means. In a serial arrangement, the bits are sent one after another along the same wire in rapid succession. This has become the more common interface arrangement because only 1 wire is required for a signal line rather than 8 wires. This situation is especially advantageous when the host computer and the I/O terminal are separated by long distance or when transmission is required over a telephone line. The remaining 3 conventions all involve serial transmission. They include TTL, RS232 (sometimes called EIA), and 20 milliampere current loop. You must consult the manual for your terminal or printer to see which interface is appropriate.

TTL levels

The TTL convention is the simplest but also the least common. In this arrangement the peripheral and the computer communicate with a signal that uses 0 volts as a logic 0 (a space) and +5 volts as a logic 1 (a mark). These are the same logic levels used in the Sinclair. For this interface, you may simply connect the transmit data (Pin 6) and the receive data (Pin 2) of the 6850 directly to the peripheral. For the dumb-terminal operation, the transmit data line connects to the keyboard input line of the host computer or modem while the receive data line connects to the printer or display. Finally you must connect the signal grounds from the host and the Sinclair together as well, making a third wire in the interface. If you are interfacing to a printer, you will only need the transmit data line and a ground.

RS232 levels

The second, and by far the most common, serial convention is the RS232 or EIA. In this convention, a mark is -12 volts while a space is $+12$ volts. The best way to establish these logic levels is to use the 1488 and 1489 level shifters (pin-outs in Fig. 11.1) hooked up as shown in Figure 11-2. Note that both a positive and a negative supply are needed for the RS232 interface. A suitable unregulated supply is shown in Figure 11-3. If you are simply interfacing to an RS232 printer, then the 1489 circuit will not be necessary, since the received data line is only used in the dumb-terminal application.

RS232 systems generally use a standard connector as well. It is a 25-pin subminiature connector usually listed as an RS232 type. If you are interfacing to a printer, then you will want the female connector on the Sinclair end. Put the transmit signal on Pin 3 and the ground on Pin 7. If, on

FIGURE 11-1
Data for MC1488 and MC1489. Courtesy Motorola
Semiconductor Products, Inc.

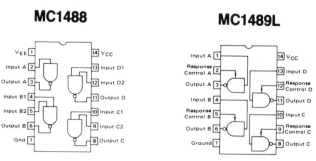

FIGURE 11-2
Schematic for the RS232 level shifter

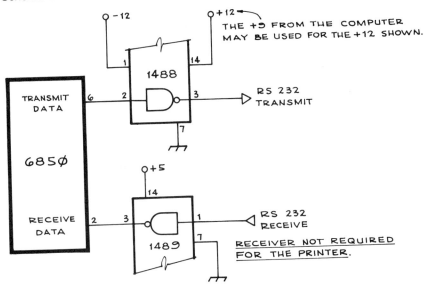

FIGURE 11-3
A power supply for the level shifters. The unregulated outputs are suitable for either the current loop or the RS232 level shifters described here. CAUTION: The 110-volt section of this circuit is extremely dangerous. Be sure all 110-volt wires are properly insulated.

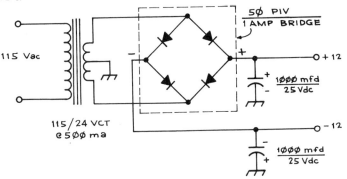

the other hand, you are implementing the dumb terminal, then you should use the male connector, since the Sinclair is now the peripheral rather than the host. Put the receive line on Pin 3 and the transmit line on Pin 2. Pin 7 is again ground. Checking Pins 2 and 3 of both devices with a voltmeter is a safe practice *before* connection is made. A device's transmit line will show a negative voltage; the receive line will show none.

137

20 milliampere current loop

The last serial convention we will cover is the 20 milliampere current loop. This is the oldest of the conventions and is found primarily on the old ASR 33 Teletypes. This system is based on mechanical relays opening and closing. The open-circuit condition is a space, while the closed-circuit condition represents a mark. The ASR 33 Teletypes make fine printers and are quite cheap. They run at 110 baud (which is 10 characters per second) and use inexpensive paper. Two types of current loop driver circuits will be presented here.

Current loop devices are either active or passive. The active side supplies the voltage to establish the current loop. Thus, for any 20 ma current loop connection one side must be active and the other must be passive. If you plan to connect your Sinclair to another current loop device, you must first determine whether that device is active or passive so that you can configure the Sinclair to complement that device. The determination can easily be done with the aid of a volt-ohm meter. Put the meter on a 0-100 milliampere scale and connect it across the 2 *signal input* lines to that device. If the meter indicates 0 current, the input is passive. If a current of approximately 20 milliamperes is observed then the input is active. Next connect the meter to the 2 output signal lines. When the device is not sending data the meter will read 0 regardless of whether it is active or passive. When characters are sent, however, a current deflection of 5 to 10 ma will be observed if the device is active. Usually, teletypes and other printers will be passive, similarly, most computers and modems will be active.

If you are building the printer only, then the active transistor circuit shown in Figure 11-4 will suffice. The advantage of this circuit is that only +5 volts are needed to key the printer. If you are building a dumb terminal and you need to interface to a 20 milliampere line, then we suggest one of the circuits shown in Figure 11-5. Although a 5-volt supply will key a teletype, we find that at least 12 volts is required to complete the read loop. The old-fashioned relays are replaced in this circuit by Darlington optoisolators. The ±12 volt supply shown in Figure 11-3 will be needed if the active version of the circuit is required. Note that the negative side of the read and transmit loops can be tied together in either the active or the passive versions to make a 3 wire connection.

FIGURE 11-4
A simple current-loop transmitter for use with the printer

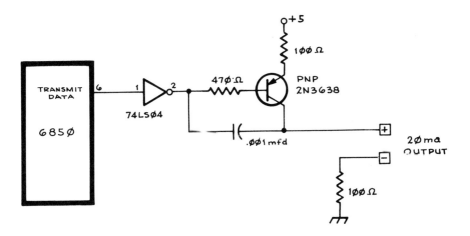

FIGURE 11-5
Bidirectional current loop. Optoisolators replace
old-fashioned relays.

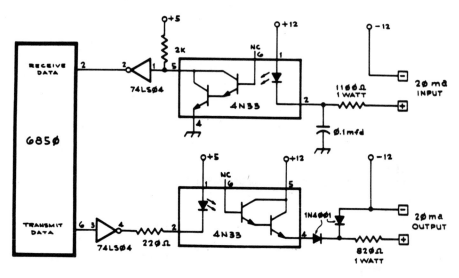

ACTIVE

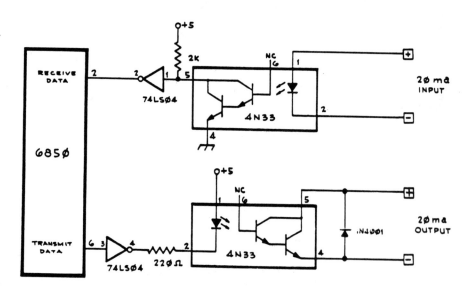

PASSIVE

INDEX

141